DEDICATION

To Michael Cowan known affectionately as Moo Cow. Your understanding of what the Dragon School stood for and your ability to articulate this has been a great help. We are all so sorry you are not with us to enjoy this book.

A Sense of Purpose

By

Bev MacInnes

Edited by Graham Sawyer and Janette Ryan

A.C.U.P./Anglo Anzus Publications

PREFACE

I am very pleased to be asked to write a preface to *A Sense of Purpose.* The Dragon has always thrived because it has been able not only to attract good staff but has allowed them to remain characters and his former colleagues and pupils will know that Bev MacInnes has certainly been a character. Histories of schools are often dull, boring and little more than a list of factual events, but *A Sense of Purpose* is very much a personal record of years spent at the Dragon, and those who were here with him will recognise the school and the people. All good schools, their teachers and their pupils very much need a sense of purpose.

Roger Trafford

ACKNOWLEDGEMENTS

The editors, Graham Sawyer and Janette Ryan, made this book possible. Their patience, understanding, probing questions and suggestions were crucial.

Anthony Cree provided invaluable support throughout this project, with his experience and knowledge of education in England and Australia.

Vicki Conrad, my Secretary, spent many hours and showed a high level of professionalism in putting the book together, and Heather Thomas who helped in the final weeks of the project.

Yasmin Hollis took on the job of designing the cover.

Tim Heeney, an Old Boy of the Dragon School, and a Lawyer in Toronto, kindly acted for us and carefully read the script to ensure it was all correct legally.

My thanks to John Madden, Enid Volak, Janet Murphy, Alexis Troubetzkoy, Margaret Needler and Sandy Heard for reading the script and making useful comments.

Thanks too to Jonathan Grosvenor for helping with the epilogue and other suggestions about how best to distribute and sell the book in England.

Beryl Payne, a former student who lived in Sept Iles for the whole of her schooling, kindly contributed a section to this book describing the highlights of pioneering life in the early days of the iron ore development in that part of Quebec and Labrador.

I used the Dragon School Magazine "The Draconian", which comes out three times a year, as a major source of material. I read and took notes from ninety issues, and I thank particularly those who wrote the amusing, accurate and stimulating notes on each term: Chris Jaques (Jacko), John Clark (Clarkie), Douglas Dalrympie (Dougie), Roland Marshall (Roly), and Tony Kelly. "The Dragon Century" (1877 to 1977) by Chris Jaques was a valuable source.

My thanks too to Tony Thorn and David Andrew for help with the Sing Song and to Cindy Smith for descriptive details.

Although they did not help with the writing of the book, I thank David Parnell (Parni) and Robin Houghton (Lofty). So much I describe in the book was made possible by them, their leadership, advice and hard work behind the scenes.

John Dizer (Dizzy) and Chris Cutcliffe (Cigi) with their reconnaissance, pioneering, planning and knowledge of local footpaths, made possible the variety of walks which we undertook.

I thank also Noelle Oke who supplied me with newsletters and magazines from the Scots School, Albury in Australia.

CONTENTS

LIST OF PHOTOGRAPHS

INTRODUCTION

My years at the Dragon School, Oxford were important to myself and to the School.

This School is a national institution and this is a credit to Skipper, Hum and Joc Lynam as well as Keith Ingram (Inky) and Michael Gover (Guv). I was privileged to have had Joc, Inky and Guv as my Headmasters. I am also grateful to Phil Doddridge, Principal at Sept Iles, Quebec, and to John Edwards, Head of the Primary School at the Scots School, Albury.

I hope I described the Dragon, a unique, unconventional and great school, so that the reader can understand its qualities. All those studying and working at the School did do with a strong "sense of purpose". I was given the opportunity to do many things, and to try new things. I describe it all as I saw it. Don't imagine for one moment that I was the only person doing so. There were colleagues more able than I who made greater contributions.

The point is that the children at the School came first, certainly above the wishes of adults and way above administration. Such a book may imply that the author is vain. I am sorry if this appears to be so but I can only describe events with which I was in some way connected. The story is in no way a school history. There are whole areas of great importance which I either leave out or I give only cursory consideration to their importance.

If there are any profits from the sales of the book, they will be donated to educational charities.

CHAPTER 1

First Arrival

In 1961, I set about finding work in a school in England. During the summer I visited over twenty schools. I had come from Canada with no idea or understanding of all the various schools, State, Direct Grant or Independent. One day in late June I drove into Oxford, asked directions and parked on St Margaret's Road. I well remember as the trees have burls on them and later as I drove away there was a scratch the length of the car. I had to pay to have it repaired.

I set out to find the Dragon School. This part of North Oxford contains many large houses with colleges never far away. I walked down Bardwell Road (I call the short, two block road, the Bardwell Road from now on, as it was the title of a song Joc sang at the Sing Song - more about that later). Oxford was a city of about one hundred and fifty thousand with its famous University and much industry, particularly in the motor trade. North Oxford, protected on its sides by the Cherwell River and Port Meadow, was where many of the "Dons" (college Professors and Lecturers) lived.

I asked where the Dragon School was. There was no sign. I was directed towards a building called School House. It was a long brick building with wings at either end. There seemed to be a certain buzz around the School. I hesitated and looked across the Bardwell Road opposite School House. It was the middle of the day and the boys (I later discovered a few girls too) were mainly out on the fields. I watched from the pavement leaning on the

1

picket fence. Right in front of me there were cricket nets, several of them. Some staff, bats in hand, were demonstrating the off drive and square cut. Others bowled at boys batting. There were at least four boys in each net and the action was purposeful and continuous. No one seemed to get hurt. Further out I could see games of cricket and in the distance, tennis. Very far away to my left were figures in swimming gear and the noise of splashing and laughter. Everyone seemed to be having a good time.

I was early so I had a few minutes to take in the scene before crossing the road and approaching School House. One entrance had a partly opened door and a bell. I rang, nothing happened, so I went inside. I walked down a corridor and cried out, "Anyone here?" I thought this best as the doors I tried led to empty rooms. Eventually a tall young man appeared who, due to his height, I later learned, was called Lofty. I said that I had an appointment. He replied that the Headmaster was not available. I had, prudently as it turned out, kept a letter which he had sent me in Canada. It gave a date and time, clearly the Headmaster had to be found!

I was put in the drawing room and told to wait. I always found this room, which I got to know well, a very relaxed, bright and friendly place. There were comfortable stuffed chairs with attractive covers. On one side there was a glass case containing silver and blue china with a Dragon motif. In the corner by the door was a corner cabinet that I discovered held drinks. There was below it a walnut table that could be folded out to provide a place on which to put trays of tea. Above the fireplace were two flowering plants on stands and vases of roses. There was coal port china on a shelf. At the far end of the room a couple of substantial clocks ticked away. The carpets were thick and clean and the curtains full-length. There were pillows on top of the radiators all low enough to sit on. Five tall windows let in light and pointed east, south and west. The School House was built at the turn of the century and had been designed by the Headmaster's grandfather who was an architect. I sat in a chair that looked out on a driveway, flowerbeds full of roses and a lawn. The latter was in use as a grass tennis court, marked out, with a tennis net and further netting ten feet high at each end to prevent tennis balls going too far. Children and adults came and went along the driveway, mostly into the other entrance at the far end of the house that must have been at least three hundred feet long. A gong sounded and the hum of voices immediately stopped.

Somewhat flustered, the Headmaster arrived, full of apologies. He was a very striking man with white hair, well but not over-dressed, wearing a sweater, jacket and tie. He walked with a slight limp as he had an arthritic hip. From somewhere in the back reaches of the building an instant lunch, a pork pie and salad on a plate, were produced. He offered to pour me a gin and tonic from the bar in the corner cupboard. I chose a tomato juice as I was driving back to Windsor where I was staying.

He had much charm. He introduced himself as Joc Lynam and explained that his father Hum, and uncle Skipper, had been headmasters before him. He told me that there were five hundred boys, half of whom boarded. Day boys started in a baby (junior) school at age seven and the first boarders came at age eight. There had always been a few day girls including his sister Audrey. After five years in this prep school, most took exams to get into secondary schools known as public schools. He said that he was lucky to have an excellent staff, many of whom had been at the

School for a long time. They found Oxford pleasant and the School was great fun, even if they all worked very hard. He was especially emphatic on this point. The staff were very committed. He told me that the School year was divided into three terms, school started in September and finished in late July.

I supposed we talked for half an hour. I had submitted a resumé (curriculum vitae) when I had first written to him. He rose suddenly from his chair saying that I would have to come back and asking me to leave my whereabouts with his secretary. And then he was gone.

I visited a number of schools that summer, some quite interesting, but I had decided that the Dragon School was for me. At most other schools, the "chemistry" was wrong. Either I could hear adults shouting at children, or I passed lines of children standing or walking in grim silence. At that time there was a great shortage of Science graduates applying to schools. Heads tended to go into long job descriptions and not to offer much other information. It all seemed rather humourless. At one remote school I had been asked to turn up for lunch. On the way I lost myself in a maze of unfenced roads high on the moors. I arrived forty five minutes late to be told by the Headmaster's wife that this was unacceptable. I left without an interview or lunch.

Three weeks later I returned to the Dragon School. At that time the summer term continued until the end of July. I had been told I should spend a couple of days at the School and I was put up in a home nearby. I was put in the charge of three members of staff during that time: Chris, John H. and Denny. Little did I know that my future prospects lay in their hands!

For two days I attended morning assembly, lessons, bun break (recess), games, meals and activities. Some of the time boys were guides. I was impressed when one boy took me to his garden, a kind of allotment right in the middle of the School. There he had planted an assortment of petunias, marigolds and radishes. They all seemed to be doing very well.

What impressed me most were the lessons. They were all lively, interesting (remember it was very near the end of the school year so a certain amount of academic pressure was off) and had a purpose. The interplay between the children and the teachers was new to me. It was at times bedlam, but the teachers were always in control. When asked to take out their compasses and draw a circle of two inches in diameter, they all did it with a minimum of fuss. At that time my experience of schools was limited. When I was doing my Diploma of Education course I had visited at least a dozen schools. There the teachers tried to keep the children busy for every moment. When there were question and answer sessions, too often they got out of control. Here it all seemed so relaxed. I was particularly impressed that at the end of lessons there was a breezy repartee between staff and children.

In the evenings I met other staff, matrons and "stooges". The matrons looked after the boys who were boarding. They got them up and put them to bed. They (tried!) to look after their clothes, made sure they washed, and looked after their "tuck" and teddies. They looked out for those who seemed unhappy or under stress. When, years later, I became a housemaster, good matrons really ran the boarding house. The staff, though committed and sympathetic, had many duties in the rest of the School.

The first person I met when I arrived in June was a stooge called Lofty. Over tea and at the bar I met other stooges. Years later a parent defined a stooge as: *"A Stooge is a young gentleman who is sometimes an undergraduate (college student) or sometimes waiting to be an undergraduate, who has nothing in particular to do, and can find nowhere more congenial to do it than the Dragon School."*

There were three stooges besides Lofty, and two of them became headmasters fifteen years later. To keep everything running properly at the end of the summer term, many extra hands were needed. These three stooges had finished their university term in June and were able to come to the Dragon School for six weeks as a summer job.

The matrons took me into the boarding houses and I learned that there were seven boarding houses in all. Four (with not more than twenty children) had the eight and nine year old children, one was for the ten year olds (it was larger) and two were for the eleven, twelve and thirteen year olds. I gathered that in addition there were some local school families who had a few boarders living with them.

My three minders made sure that I was fully occupied. The one area I didn't see was Science, as the man who ran all the Science was away and he was leaving at the end of term. Lofty did show me the Science Room which was well-equipped.

When it was time to go I told Joc, the Headmaster, that this was where I wanted to teach. He was friendly, even enthusiastic, but non-committal. Again I told his charming secretary, Barbara, where I could be found in the coming weeks. The Headmaster said that he would touch base first with Chris, John H., Denny and perhaps some matrons and stooges. It shows how thorough they were at interviewing me. My background was not British, nor had I been at one of the better-known southern hemisphere public schools like Bishops in Cape Town or Melbourne Grammar.

I politely declined all other offers as I felt I had a good chance and if it didn't come through then I would go back to Canada where I knew I could get a job in a school or industry, as a graduate chemical engineer.

Sometime in August, shortly after the Berlin Wall went up, I was touring with friends in Norway. When we reached a small hotel on the Sognefiord there was a telegram waiting

"Expect you twentieth September"

Signed Joc

I had passed the scrutiny!

I now thought back to my past as a boy and as a teacher. Could I possibly be ready for the fray?

As a boy aged ten I remember one experience above all others. This could be useful as I would be teaching ten year olds. In a very hot August week during the war, I drew and painted trains in a room in the basement of the Montreal Museum of Fine Art. Arthur Lismer, the Museum Director, had a room full of children painting long trains and I was especially keen on the caboose at the train's rear. He helped with paintings and drawings. At the end we rolled up the drawings and took them home to spread out on our bedroom walls. He was such a nice man and was on his hands and knees with us. For years I conspired to get my parents to go to level crossings to see, I hoped, a caboose.

My start as a teacher came more than forty years ago. I had decided to take up teaching after taking a degree in Engineering at

McGill University in Montreal. I was lucky to be given the opportunity to do some work for the Protestant School Board in Montreal as a supply teacher.

I knew nothing about teaching, but you learn fast when put in front of a class. That is when a good many decide teaching isn't for them. The following year I enrolled in Education at Bishops University in Lennoxville, eighty miles east of Montreal. The course was excellent, and was run by Dr. Jefferis (known as Jeff), who set very high standards. He was very much an academic, well read, a good actor on stage (and off!), and a character. His wife was very understanding as we made fun of Jeff and his dog Guinness. His course was very demanding. We had lectures and studied theory in the morning, and in the afternoons we were sent to teach in various schools. The assignments were usually for two to four weeks. There was quite a variety of schools available, from the big city high school in nearby Sherbrooke, to small one-room schools containing several grades in the room, deep in the townships to the east.

Jeff might turn up at any time to observe. He could be quite outspoken about us the following day. We had to dress properly and the ladies must not appear to be attention seeking from their appearance. He made us prepare our lesson plans properly, encouraged us to depart from simply following the syllabus in text books, and to use visual aids.

Above all we were told to stand during lessons, speak clearly, and write on the blackboard legibly without turning our back to the class for too long. It wasn't easy, but it was very good advice.

We had to learn to adapt. I was first sent to teach senior French at a local boarding school. There was nothing in my background to indicate I could cope with this. Unknown to Jeff, I could actually speak the language, but this wasn't a huge advantage. Ron, whom I was substituting for, took me in hand and showed me all I had to know. We became lifelong friends. A fellow classmate who had majored in poetry at college had to teach junior Science at an elementary school. I stayed up in the evening to help him to rehearse his lesson plans. As there were only fifteen on the course, Jeff could visit several of us in any afternoon, and he came often. It certainly was not a course for "Prima Donnas". Many rough edges were worn off. We had twenty four weeks of this and two three-week stints on our own in school, well away from Bishops so Jeff couldn't hover. Only when our confidence had been restored was this possible.

I won a prize. It wasn't for practice teaching, I think it was for marks overall, anyway I don't remember. For all this we received a provisional first class teaching diploma. To make this permanent, we had to teach for two of the next three years in a provincial school somewhere in the province of Quebec. An inspector, Mr. Aikman, came to inspect us to see if we could actually teach.

I chose to go to Sept Iles. This port had been rapidly built to accommodate ships collecting iron ore brought by rail from the mines of Labrador. My family thought I chose to go there so that if it didn't work out then no one would hear about it. That wasn't accurate or fair. I lived in two rooms in a cellar with Carl, another teacher. Upstairs, Madame Frechette and her husband Johnny raised four children.

The School, the Queen Elizabeth High School, opened as I arrived. Previously the School had existed in a series of huts.

Beryl, a grade ten student in 1959, now a teacher, added the following description. With her background of living there from the beginning she reminds us all what it was like.

A Unique Experience in school at Sept Iles:

I remember the sports days at Fleming Junior School and jumping over the high jump into the sawdust; or the smell of sauerkraut upon entering the school on days when the Finnish caretaker Tony was using the school kitchen to make his own; or Carl talking to us about 'life' when our Algebra lesson for the day was over; or Shirley keeping us up to date as her romance with Tom flourished.

According to the School Annual, the Junior Students Council had a Beatnik and a skating party. I certainly remember the Beatnik party. It was great fun dressing up a la Greenwich Village, New York or Left Bank, Paris. (It must have been about that time that my friends and I dismantled our beds and put the mattresses on the floor, put candles in chianti bottles and took up poetry!) They also had fudge sales, parties and broomball games (What is broom ball? I cannot remember, but I certainly envisage brooms and a large ball and sweeping the ball into a hockey net - was this done on ice? It could be done on the playground.) Two of the students ran successful Saturday afternoon film shows to raise money. The Senior Council held a Winter Carnival according to the Annual (organised by Sheila).

Phil, our principal, did an admirable job summing up the progress of the English school since its inception. Most of the children went to French school. This was the custom in Quebec. However, he does not mention what I well remember, and that is going to the Hudson's Bay Trading Post to buy textbooks as we had to when we arrived in 1952. The old trading post had snowshoes hanging from the ceiling and while we were there an old bewhiskered trapper came in for supplies. Alas, it was replaced a few months ago, if not weeks later by a brand new Hudson's Bay shop which had none of the character of the old one.

The School supported the Red Cross through fund raising successfully; a music club was begun; a successful model of a General Assumbly of the United Nations was held; we also debated a motion regarding the merits of communism versus capitalism and the motion favoring communism won; a Christmas tree sale and tea and bake sale provided funds for a class Christmas party; a play was presented for an assembly; money raising schemes included a baby sitting service, a Saturday car wash to pay for the class trip to Schefferville; the candidates for the student's council were introduced to the School at a candidates dance (called a candid dance); the beatnik party was held at the elementary school with "real gone art", blue lights and slow jazzy music; there was a Sadie Hawkins Dance when the 'gals' hauled their men off to Marryin Sam; the Winter Carnival included a broom ball game - teachers versus students, a sleigh ride and a dance; there was a hockey game against neighbouring Port Cartier followed by a prom and a Queen of the Carnival. There was a Valentines Dance and a visit to Port Cartier for hockey games and basketball games with dances afterwards. We attended an Easter Dance at the RCAF base and the RCAF DJs appear to have provided music not only for this but for the Valentines Dance as well.

Although sports was dominated by curling there was also hockey and basketball. We played against both local and teams from Port Cartier. The Juniors had hockey teams and baseball teams and they also enjoyed a tincan bonspiel.

1959 was a very exciting year. The new high school opened. It was built at company expense to educate the manager's children to university level standard and nothing was stinted. There were new books and a new science laboratory equipped with Bunsen burners and new teachers; there was even a store room with jars of frogs in formaldehyde. There was a minor explosion just before the school opened when faulty gas equipment blew up which must have been a lively introduction to Bev MacInnes, our new Science teacher, who was also undertaking his first appointment.

The parents all visited the school before it opened and I was none too pleased to be embarrassed by Mr. MacInnes telling the class how my father had chased my mother around the school with a dead snake!

Nevertheless, the school was a far cry from the early days of education in Sept Iles when the English children attended school at Mile Three - the construction camp outside of town where the men, and some families, lived in prefabricated plywood huts and where they also played. The four junior grades used the one-roomed church as a school house. While across the dirt highway to the airport the older children moved aside beer bottles to do their sums in the social rooms that comprised the OUR club (Ore Ungava Railway).

However, progress was swift and by 1954 the English speaking Catholics and Protestants had already been segregated at either end of the town block separated by the sea of sand which became their playground. The one-storey protestant school was soon too small and so in 1959 the older children moved to Queen Elizabeth Intermediate School - intermediate because it only went up to grade 11.

Being educated in a boom town is not without benefits. We may not have had access to libraries, art galleries, museums or theatres, but the Iron Ore Company was determined that the children of their employees should be given a good academic education. There were no frills: no art or music or drama.

However, we were encouraged to have senior and junior student councils with vigorously fought elections for positions. The Council organised a school shop to sell stationary and sports equipment. A Publishing Committee produced a school year book at the end of the year and a newspaper was produced. The Council organised the sports teams and fixtures. Delegates were sent to the Annual Convention. A Constitution was adopted and a school crest was designed. Money was raised to finance all these activities through dances, film shows, and sale of goods.

All this was accomplished even though school numbers were very low. Our first yearbook shows one graduate. However the second year there were twelve. It was like attending private school.

The Social Committee ran several successful dances; each themed with elaborate decorations. Once the school hall was turned into a French café complete with striped awnings and café tables. Another time, huge stars were made by threading strings through straws which were then sprayed silver and hung from the ceiling.

None of these activities would have been possible without the encouragement and active involvement of our teachers who *inspired us and gave of their time and energy freely.*

The Canadian education system imposed a rigid uniformity which had the advantage that if your family had to move across the country the chances were that your new school would be using the same textbook and be more or less on the same page as the school you had left. This left you to concentrate on making new friends. However, some teachers used their own initiative to liven up lessons. Year 11 must have caused some disturbance to other classes when they dropped items from the first floor window to test the effect of gravity on the speed of different items.

Sept Iles was called "The Land God Gave Cain" by Jacques Cartier when he set foot on its shores in 1492 and Hammond Innes has written a book by the same name. It is well deserved. The winters are long and cold but dry with brilliant sunsets reflecting against whiter than white snow. Although there were primitive ski slopes outside of town only the truly dedicated took to them. Curling on natural ice indoors at the OUR Club had become a very popular sport among adults and teenagers alike although weekends long bonspiels left us rather exhausted on Monday mornings.

We had access to a new sports centre which was built across the road from the school where we learned a rather athletic form of rock 'n roll from the resident P.E. teacher.

The pupils at the school were a very mixed bunch with widely differing backgrounds. Many adults had come to Sept Iles to make a fresh start after the war so we had a smattering of nationalities as well which you probably would not have had in small town Canada at the time.

Beryl's father worked at the ore terminal. The children's families all worked in Sept Iles or further up the rail line. Another student, Joan, was the daughter of the manager, and Sheila, was the daughter of a railway man. They came from every background as their parents had come to this new frontier to start life again and to seek their fortune.

I taught a large variety of Science and Mathematics subjects as well as Geography and History for grades ten and eleven. There were provincial Matriculation exams for both grades. Those who could afford it continued after grade eleven to technical school or university. The classes were small, less than twenty. I had to work very hard at preparation to keep up.

I took my first school expedition, by train, four hundred miles north to Shefferville to see the iron ore mines and the Labrador plain. It is so cold that it takes a fir tree fifty years to grow six feet high. Tony, our Finnish janitor, had built a sauna next to his house. On Friday evenings he asked a group of friends, including the School Principal Phil, and me to join him. It was a good way to steam away the troubles of the week just passed.

On a calm, clear day in May in my second year there, we measured the speed of sound along a magnificent beach on the Gulf of St Lawrence. Parents accompanied grades ten and eleven with rifles, stop watches, flags and binoculars. It worked perfectly as there was no wind and we were at sea level.

The children did well in their Matriculation exams. The Inspector, Mr. Aikman was pleased so I was ready to leave. I only learnt about the Dragon School because Mary, a teacher at Roedean College in England, visited us. She was on a scholarship from the Royal Geographic Society to investigate aspects of mining and shipping iron ore. When I heard she was coming, I asked my classes if anyone would have her to stay. Several hands shot up, and Sheila was so proud to have her stay with her family. Mary had driven trucks (lorries) during the war and a friend from those days had two boys at the Dragon School. Her friend, Ann, wrote to Joc Lynam on my behalf and that is how I came to be introduced to the Dragon School.

1. Graduating Class, Queen Elizabeth High School, 1961

CHAPTER 2

The Start

I duly presented myself at the Dragon School on 20 September. No one was about. Alice in the School House kitchens took me in hand, cooked meals for me, and found me a bed for two nights until the School showed signs of starting. I was soon introduced to Joc's study. This was a very special place and quite different from the drawing room at the other end of the School House. The desk was against the wall so the Headmaster would never be interviewing anyone from behind it. Even at the start of the term, there were vast piles of papers in several layers on the desk. There was a bar in a far corner with boxes of glasses and soft drinks to go with the spirits which were locked away in the cupboard. There was a sink in one corner, an umbrella stand behind the door, and a stand for cigarette butts. There were only three chairs and a vast bureau with several small pull-out drawers containing pens and special kinds of paper as well as sweets, bottle openers, various tools, scissors and a stapler. There was usually a pile of newspapers on a table and many family and team photos on the wall. It was very much a room that was "lived in", and from memory, it was twenty feet square. The lighting was good, especially over the desk.

Joc had a constant stream of people who came to see him. They included the Bishop of Oxford, a local gardener discussing weed control and management of the boys' allotments, a friend dropping by with racing tips, and a young lady braving the male-dominated scene and determined to come to teach at the School. All were made to feel welcome and that they were important to him.

Joc had an instinct for finding good staff, and he was nearly always right. Many years later I met Tim, by then Headmaster of a large school in Australia. When he was in his early twenties he had been touring England with a cricket side that had been playing at a ground not far from the School. A local friend asked him out to supper but first the friend had to collect something from Joc's study.

Tim and his friend duly presented themselves and stayed for a drink. There were others present. Tim talked with Joc, he said he might stay at the end of the tour, and did Joc have any suggestions as to where he might find a job on a construction site or in a pub. They said their farewells.

"Just a minute," said Joc, "I think I might have something which might interest you!" He took Tim's phone number. Later Tim, who had not thought particularly about teaching, gave him a ring. Soon Tim returned to the Bardwell Road and the start of a most successful teaching career.

Most staff were hired for who they were, their attitude, interest, and enthusiasm, as well as having a good academic background. Oxford was a most attractive place to live and work.

Children came into the study from time to time if Joc was there. He might be telling them off, but more likely they would come to borrow something. Along the wall in his study or in a cupboard next door he had an array of Joc cricket bats, Joc tennis rackets, Joc tins of tennis balls, Joc rugger and soccer balls, Joc hockey sticks and even Joc bikes for stooges. I asked him if he was always satisfied that they all came back. He said of course, they were all properly marked.

Stooges were important to Joc. As well as all the jobs around the School, from taking attendance, to washing, repairing and blowing up rugger and soccer balls, they had to keep Joc supplied with everything: drink, the Racing Times, other papers, and stationery, and they collected notes written to him by staff and letters he wrote. Later, when I ran the Christmas Charity sale, I was always glad to have at least one sale stooge who was prepared to do almost anything, particularly the physical moving of goods, tables and so on, which I could not have done alone.

The door was almost always ajar and staff could come in to discuss matters, or later in the evening to socialise. In this way there were far fewer formal interviews with staff than at many schools. All of us kept him in touch and up to date.

So far I haven't said much about the children. Now I was thrown in at the deep end. Everything was so strange, and once the staff meeting was over, the pace of events was unlike anything I had ever known.

First I had to come to grips with the teaching of Science. I taught something like twelve different classes in a week. The Science room was admirably equipped with pretty well all the basic needs. There was electricity, gas and water. I devised a series of demonstration lessons in basic Chemistry, electricity, magnetism, pressure and so on. I had been given no syllabus and no one else taught Chemistry and Physics. An excellent Biology teacher taught lower down the School. I had a different approach for each of the three age groups.

As well there was a Science Club. Lofty, apart from being a stooge, worked towards a Science degree at Oxford University. He was able to come to the School some evenings to help me get started with the Science Club. His help was invaluable. The Club had been a very busy, inspiring, creative and popular one under my predecessor. Cosmo seemed to be in charge. This thirteen year old boy made the transition very easy for me. Radio-controlled models continued to be built.

When a boy first joined the Club, there was a series of experiments on index cards, each of which had to be passed, before going on to the next. Some were ingenious. A smoke box was lit, filled with smoke and a ray of light passed through. The ray could be bent by lenses and prisms. I resisted cigarettes as a source of smoke and stuck to smoldering cardboard. Once a number of sets (four out of seven I think) had been mastered, then the boy could try to build something on his own. The Science room was too small for a whole class to do experimental or practical work, even in pairs, so this was a good introduction, something which couldn't be done in lessons.

The Science Club was very loyal and helped to repair and set up demonstrations. I was greatly helped by a local school which had a larger laboratory and lent me, when I needed it, a vacuum pump and static electricity producer called a Wimshurst machine. At least twice a year I went to London, visited bookstores, suppliers and toy shops. Once on a whim I called at the Soviet Embassy. This was not long after both Yuri Gagarin and John Glenn had been sent into space. We lived in the Sputnik era. I was lucky, the Ambassador was expecting a visit from someone and I matched his description. I was immediately ushered into his presence by an aide. He soon found out I was someone else and he treated it as a huge joke. No vodka was offered, but a cultural attaché was told to fix me up. In this way I acquired, on loan, a wonderful propaganda film about the first Russian trip into space. I was thrilled and so were the children.

It was a wonderful experience to be let loose on one's own to produce lessons, run a voluntary Science Club and not to have syllabi imposed or have exams as the main object. The reason that there was no set syllabus was quite simply because it wasn't yet considered a subject ready to be tested by outside examiners. I did of course help scholarship candidates by giving them a bit of scientific background where needed. These exams were carefully prepared and often the answer lay in data given with the questions. I did give tests from time to time to see how the classes kept up with the demonstration lessons and each boy or girl had a notebook.

At this time one intervention very much impressed me. The producer of the school play suddenly came into the Science Club carrying a huge board with all the rehearsals. Bruno had been doing the plays for over forty years, but he still came to me in first term to make sure that there was no friction between Science Club and rehearsals. I never forgot that, especially many years later when I produced a play.

I was also assigned two sets of children for Mathematics, as well as one for Geography, and another for History. As these seemed to take place in different classrooms every day, I was pressed to be able to turn up at all.

I knew nothing of English History. I was given a book to start with, so I made up my own lessons about cowboys, Indians, and

Mounties on the Prairies. Years later I discovered that Martin, a boy in this first (and my last!) History class, during a two week period, had been ill for one lesson, at the doctor for a second, at a music lesson for the third, and had to face a test for the fourth lesson. He had done very badly and on a fortnightly report (we reported every two weeks at this time) I had written, "Martin needs to pay more attention in class."

His parents were furious, quite rightly. I didn't yet know the children, nor clearly had I taken attendance. Someone in authority protected me. If this sort of mistake had been repeated, no doubt I would have heard about it. I was only just beginning to get some confidence and this was recognised by those in authority. Not that I was protected in other ways. Once when I was rushed and tired I read my mail (or post) during a meal when I should have been supervising the serving of food and the manners. I received a sharp note.

The Mathematics classes were difficult. Mathematics was grouped into sets by ability and I was given two sets, of average range of two age levels. For a couple of weeks I really struggled. After the first week I knew where to go myself for each lesson. There was a five-minute interval between lessons so staff and children could get from one lesson to the next. The boys, taking advantage of this, went into the playground and played with their marbles. Pyramids were set up, big semis (a type of marble) swapped for something more exotic, with books, pens etc thrown down in a corner.

The second bell rang which signalled the start of the lesson. Marbles were swiftly stuffed into pockets and special bags, books and pens retrieved, at least some of them, and put in pockets. Only then was it time to even figure out where to go. For several minutes boys wandered and ran into the class. I remonstrated to no avail.

One day I picked up a gym shoe left by someone on a row of hooks by the door and hit the last boy to appear once very hard on the bottom. There was a hush. Absolute silence. From then onward the lessons went like clockwork, suddenly I seemed to have arrived. Boys came up to me at the end of a lesson to briefly chat. Previously all I got was a sort of salute as they rushed out. Now they waited to be dismissed rather than try to rush the door before I had finished.

I even came to an understanding concerning marbles dropped during a lesson. They could be reclaimed next time. At last there was some order and we could start to teach and learn. It was all a far cry from the excellent, well controlled, but lively lessons I had seen when being interviewed. With the help of Ticks, a very senior master, I developed a routine for the start of each lesson. Ten items of mental arithmetic to be done in notebooks or at least the answers recorded, starting thirty seconds after the bell.

The children had, putting it bluntly, to be made to work and produce results, at least until I was established. Only then could one start to relax and enjoy the teaching. One made one's own discipline. Help was always at hand and every suggestion and assistance available, but in the end it was up to me.

Text books were slightly frowned upon. True, there were sets of these available (in Mathematics), but they never quite followed the syllabus. It was therefore necessary to draw up one's own lessons and plans from topics on the list. On demand, those who had taught for some time would add detail, particularly at the level of difficulty expected. I learnt to never throw anything away, it might come in useful another time. Homework assignments, known as prep, were set out on sheets, copied on Gestetner or Banda and handed out.

Prep was assigned twice per week, with notebooks collected, corrected and returned promptly. The School demanded that children be ranked in core subjects on the basis of marks taken at two week intervals. A fortnightly report was written by me on each child (except in Science). This was a way for me to check that meaningful activity was taking place in lessons.

In time this kind of reporting was amended and five sets of very comprehensive written reports substituted, still with the same orders. The first of these were written to coincide with the initial half term in late October. Whatever one said was scrutinized closely by Headmaster, housemasters and parents.

A parent commented once that the reports were a charming way of getting to know the staff. By this he meant that we were encouraged to put down what we really thought about each child, no hiding behind noncommittal phrases. Too often these days reporting is channelled in such a way that it becomes almost an exercise in ticking the boxes, and the real reporting never takes place. Some teachers, including me, were sometimes guilty of expecting too much. Those in authority soon were aware of this. Sometimes they were pleased and after a remark about lack of effort they might say that Little Johnny could and should do better as clearly he was not being fully stretched. Parents and housemasters could take the opposite view, namely that Little Johnny was miserable in the boarding house or at home, and couldn't I lay off a bit and he would work better under less pressure. In other words, reports could be quite useful as it kept us all in touch with each other. On the other hand, one could duck by saying that Johnny was making "fair progress", or "coming along quite well". This might on the other hand indicate slackness in the classroom on the part of the teacher.

The "piece de resistance" came with exams towards the end of the first term. The same exam was set for a group of two or three adjacent sets or forms. If you had the middle set, then one was more able and the other less, and this should be reflected in the results. Agreement was reached on the syllabus covered, and an outside examiner set, marked and wrote a report on the exam. This outside examiner was a colleague who taught the same subject. All the names in order of marks were set down on a long sheet. This was then handed up for comments which were usually positive, but sometimes there was criticism. "Not a good result for Mr. M's set." These comments and results were posted in a public place where staff, children and parents could read them. Soon after I arrived they were put in a common room box instead. It certainly kept the teachers up to the mark, but I wonder how much good, if any, the whole exercise was for the children.

It all worked fairly well. Each child had a form teacher who took them for at least one major subject. Parents largely kept their distance and didn't interfere, but in cases of distress they knew that there was someone to approach.

One day I met a friend, who was very positive in many ways, but she had been very pushy about her daughter's progress during her time with us. She was always manoeuvring to have the girl placed into a higher set or form. She thought the faster pace and higher standards would help her to win a scholarship at a well known public school. Not only did her daughter fail in the scholarship exams, but she was made to take the school's entry test. This was unusual as candidates normally did well enough to gain entry even if the scholarship was too demanding. The mother was furious, but the system had to be allowed to work. Each child should be allowed to find his or her own level, if this had happened in the case of this girl, she would have passed into the school easily through the entry test in the first place.

Games were new to me. In my previous school all games were coached by the physical education staff. At the Dragon School, every able-bodied teacher, certainly those younger than fifty, and in some cases well beyond, was expected to take part. An exception was made for the ladies, at least until the number of girls increased so that there were separate girls' games. Until then, the girls played games with the boys and sometimes with distinction. For some games girls were excused.

As a boy I had played soccer, so I wondered how I would manage to cope with rugby. I needn't have worried. I was assigned to help Denny, and he certainly kept things moving, so there was no time for boredom. All the boys changed in a very confined changing room. There were at the most, twenty minutes between the end of lessons and the start of practice.

The children were all placed in one of four groups and within the group played in a game where all were more or less the same standard. The weather during September and October was ideal, so the practices were able to be undertaken routinely. We all played or took games at least three times a week and two of the sessions took place at lunch time, thereby breaking up the academic day, and taking advantage of better weather and light, particularly by November. The older and more able boys played in elite groups, and in matches against other schools.

It was possible to promote or demote boys to a higher or lower game and, hopefully, this was accomplished during the first month. The boys then got used to playing with one another in practices and inter-games matches. We played each of the other groups twice, so out of roughly thirty game sessions, only six were inter-games. The boys learned to play as a team and not just as a group of individuals. Results of games, even at the inter-school level, were not taken too seriously. The reputation of the School never depended on the results. Certainly there was praise for teams and individual performances, but it was never overdone. Some staff took the group games results very seriously, an attitude which was laughed at by other staff and sometimes the children too.

Duties were many, and varied. Changing rooms, patrol, dormitory, weekends and further patrols. Those are my memories of the early years.

No duties are always fun, but the evening dormitory duty came close. I was taken in on one night per week by Ian and Meg, the housemaster and his wife. They had very small children, so when I arrived at 6.30pm the little ones were usually in bed. The boarders, sixteen if I remember, did supervised prep down at the School and then arrived suddenly in a bunch. They washed their hands and got ready for supper. There was often a short prayer for starters. After stacking the plates and cutlery, the duty pair would wash down the tables and then they all went upstairs to get ready for bed. The housemaster and his family would retreat to their drawing room or to say goodnight to their own little ones. Sometimes they went out for a meal or to visit friends, leaving the matron, cook and dorm takers in charge.

The matron organised getting the boys ready for bed. Some had baths, some washed and all brushed their teeth and had minor sores attended to. I was supposed to maintain some sort of order. With a competent, good matron there was no need. When they were ready for bed we played a game or games. Blind Man's Buff was a favourite. I was blindfolded, and then by manoeuvring over and under the bed, had to capture a boy, correctly name him, and then he was blindfolded. This was followed by a story, such as "The Adventures of Uncle Wiggly", a story about a rabbit gentleman and his adventures. At about 8.00pm, I let them read in silence and retreated downstairs. Soon after, it was lights out with many goodnights.

The resident cook had prepared an excellent meal and I was allowed to leave when the Housemaster returned if he had been out.

This small house was home for some of the children for the first two years of boarding. All meals were eaten there and any activities, little excursions and birthdays took place there. A birthday tea was a big event in the life of a child. Adults as well as some children from outside the house attended. They were very happy occasions.

Each boy therefore had a base, and there was very much a family atmosphere. The small houses accommodated about twenty at any time which meant that everyone could come to know everyone else, and well. Parents often lived very far away so a home at school meant much both to the boy and parents. Parents sent their children away at eight years old because it was the thing to do. Now it is more and more a necessity as both parents work and jobs move them around the world. More about boarding later.

I was very much affected by a boy called Thomas. In the small house, he was lively and always at the centre of the party. He was bright and ambitious. He did well and he was never at a loss for words, fun or opinions. After he left the School, he never returned to visit. For someone who had had such a high profile that was unusual. Then one day I saw him, leaning against the same picket fence on the Bardwell Road where I had stopped briefly just before my first interview. His girlfriend did the talking. She explained that he was having a very successful career at Sandhurst and he was about to graduate near the top of his class. She had asked him to bring her to Oxford and to the School as he had talked about it. I asked them in. She thanked me, but they walked to their car and drove off. Except to say "Hello" he never spoke. I wondered about this and I do still to this day. Perhaps I was just unlucky and Thomas has returned happily on other occasions. Both he and his father are old boys. He went into all aspects of school life with such gusto and enthusiasm during his five years with us. Perhaps much of this had been a strain for him and I am sure that we would have helped had we known. Nothing will give me greater pleasure than to meet him at some future date at a school function.

Thomas's visit was a surprise but it wasn't typical. Old Dragons turned up at all times of the day. I sometimes found them following me between classes. We always tried to include them in what was happening at the moment apart from lessons and games. They came into lunch and tea and into the staff common room.

Once we had a very sad visit though we weren't to know this at the time. Duff, who was fourteen and had been with us for years prior to going on to a boarding public school, turned up one day. He arrived about the time of bun break. He hung around during games time with some of his old chums and they joined us for lunch. He was a bit evasive when questioned about how he was getting on. He said that he had the day off as a reward for extra work he had done with the school corps. When he was still around at tea we started to be concerned. Evidently he had been lent enough money by his chums and he eventually left to take a bus north to his home which was some distance away. We rang his school who had noticed he was missing and had started a search. His father met him at the bus and we later heard that his father and the school had sorted out his problems. He obviously felt at home with us and trusted us to help him.

There were dinners, open days and at the end of the Easter term, a lunch for old boys and girls then at secondary school. We led a busy life and always tried to accommodate the unexpected visitor. It showed a certain affection for the School that so many came back in this way.

About half way through the thirteen week term, I wondered when we would be paid. At the end of term I still hadn't been told, so when Edward, a school governor, came to see me, to see if he could do anything for me, I said, "Yes, could I be paid?" I received an advance within days. The governors stayed in the background and most worked very hard on behalf of the School. They left the Headmaster and staff to run the School, and as the physical plant improved, the bursar became more important.

Of course I had to offer an optional activity. Both Dizzy and I were new to the School so we set up a group calling itself "Current Affairs". We met once a week for an hour in his room. He had a tape recorder and taped items from radio news. Otherwise we relied on newspapers and prepared scrap books.

In keeping, I thought, with the relaxed approach to these activities, I wrote to an old boy of the School who was a Member of Parliament to ask him to come to see us in Dizzy's room if he was ever in Oxford. He was a controversial political figure and I had read a good deal about him.

The Headmaster ran into Humphrey, the M.P, who had arrived slightly early on the appointed day. He was very amused when told he had come to address a small group in an upstairs room. I had a note from the Headmaster to say it was fine to ask visitors, but he would like to know about it first. So it wasn't all quite as free and easy as I had thought.

Just to hold on at all during the first year was all I hoped to accomplish. When the summer term came, the pace quickened and there was more and more to cope with. An old friend, Alexis, arrived from Canada with a group of teenage children to do a summer tour of Europe, and they came to Oxford. Joc said he would like to meet him. I told Alexis where to go to find the study as I was teaching.

He arrived at the Headmaster's study on time. There were noises of sweeping, emptying of waste paper baskets, the clink of bottles and opening and closing of files. A door opened and piles of rubbish pushed against the far wall and around the corner. This would take some removing. Eventually Alexis found the courage to enter the study. A cleaner in baggy pants, and wearing two sweaters, each one full of holes, was in full gear.

"Where was the Headmaster's study and where could he find him?", asked Alexis.

"This is it and I'm he", came the reply.

Joc had formed a new friendship and Alexis would continue to visit the School over the next forty years and more.

The study was the action centre of the School. Children, staff, friends and passers-by such as Humphrey and Alexis were all made to feel welcome. Parents were interviewed in the well-appointed drawing room where I first met Joc. It was possible to make an appointment to see him during the day but that was seldom necessary. Joc went about the School during the day as much as he could to see things for himself. Special events played a vital role in determining what the School was like. In my first two years, one of these events, unplanned and unexpected, involved me in most of my non-teaching time.

During the winter of 1962 to 1963, while I was away with the Dragon in Davos Switzerland on the ski trip, it snowed in Oxford. It was at least a foot thick and it didn't melt. When we returned, it was to a winter wonderland. The river at the bottom of the School field froze after the blizzard. As I had my own skates, I spent time with friends skating to the Victoria Arms, a pub about a mile upstream. I was concerned about how it would affect the School and the routine.

I need not have worried. We all tramped down the snow on the lawn in front of the School House. Extra hoses were fitted and soon the snow, sprayed, was turning to ice. Lights were set up so spraying could go on well into the night. We were organised into relays and well supplied with whisky macs, a drink made with Stones Ginger Wine and whisky, and other medicines to keep us going. Cat ice (air bubbles under the surface) had to be eliminated. By the third day of the term there was a skatable rink and it was a good size too. The School had obtained many pairs of second-hand skates years before when a local artificial ice rink closed, to become a marmalade factory.

It being assumed that all Canadians could skate, I was able to help beginners and to suggest activities. Normal games on the field were impossible. Fortunately, I had both skates and over the years had learned to use them. Then many pairs of skates were made available to the children. By slightly altering the timetable, it was possible to give every boy and girl a chance to learn to skate. The odd chair as a support or both of my hands helped those who found it difficult to stand up. There were impromptu hockey games with bent sticks, congo lines snaked across the rink, and we played tag. It was best to keep skating in one direction or collisions were inevitable.

The water level in the river at the bottom of the field was lowered, so the covering ice tilted and broke and it became impossible for skating. The temperature rarely approached the melting point, so the ample snow on the field couldn't be made into snowballs or snowmen. Therefore these areas were not used, and instead a series of slides were built on parts of the playground. In some places there was a gradual slope. By running up to the start it was possible to glide for long distances, ending if one were going fast enough, in a boy-made snowbank. The slides were made by throwing buckets of water down and around the sliding areas. Ticks had once served in the Alpine Regiment of the British Army, and was in charge. The slides were prepared in the early evening. Cones and ropes were put out to warn off the unwary. Some pedestrians didn't pay adequate attention, and paid the inevitable price for their carelessness.

There were weekend expeditions to Blenheim Park, home of the Dukes of Marlborough, for tobogganing, and to a parental home with a large frozen pond for free-range skating. At the end of the freeze, the thaw brought floods, and put the fields out of bounds.

One good side of all the very cold weather was all the sunshine. Most days were bright and cheerful. Boys, girls, teachers, matrons, and maintenance staff were all involved. We had fun together and we all came to know each other much better.

There had been short cold spells during the previous decade and this made it possible to work out how to make the ice rink on the School house lawn. The alternative would have been very dreary. Long organised crocodile-like walks in the city parks? Crocodile walks occur when children, appropriately dressed, are taken out for exercise in poor weather or in winter conditions. They must walk single file with a teacher leading the way and another at the rear. Needless to say most children found this boring and it wasn't unusual for fights to break out towards the middle of the line, particularly if there were more than twenty children in the crocodile. We always avoided this form of exercise. Over the years I observed other schools on crocodile walks which is why I know about them.

Four years after I started, Joc retired and married his secretary Barbara. I went to teach at the Buckley School in New York City. I only stayed there a year before returning to the Dragon School.

To me Joc had represented all that an educator should be. He and his school were held in awe for what they were and for the standard achieved. He was very influential in educational circles.

In one of the many obituaries about him when he died thirteen years later, Ronnie (Yatto) wrote:

"Probably the most valuable of all the lessons which Joc taught us was that the boys (and girls) must always come first, way above their parents, way above our personal wishes or comfort, and certainly way above administration."

A former bursar, Mickey, said:

"He was not a follower of convention, he shrank from ceremony, he spurned the need for accessibility except for the boys, girls, and those working at the School. He also shunned the trappings of organisation."

There was no long list of staff with administrative titles. He did delegate, but he could and would take on the most menial task himself, if he felt that was what was needed. He was also a most genial host. He took immense trouble over the boarders' birthday teas, and he was also a genius at organising expeditions and entertainments for the staff. He played the drums with his own dance group. Much of his success came as he was a very balanced person. He had a wide range of friends and interests, from the local Railwayman's Association to horse racing. Many interests had no connection with the School.

Though I knew nothing of English schools before 1960, from what I had heard schools were too rigid. They were too concerned with order and discipline. If you were a certain sort of person then you didn't talk to most others because they were beneath you. This unconventional school was so influential because it ran well and it achieved results. Most who worked and studied there were very happy. My impression has been that in general there were far too many unhappy people in other schools. Joc attracted good staff and in return for their loyalty he didn't interfere unless he really needed to.

We were all called by our first names (or nicknames) to our face by all the boys and girls, from the most senior school prefect to a newly arrived eight year old. Joc was Joc and I was Bev. Some parents thought I was Mr. Bev. Offspring were dispatched to find out my Christian name. In return we tried to call the boys by their Christian names though many preferred Munroe and Cowan to Jeremy and Michael. Some of the nicknames of senior staff when I arrived were Spod, Box, Wilkie, Tubby, Bruno, Jacko, Ticks, Yatto and Law.

The School was enormously respected by the community and within the country. This respect was largely due to the liberal views of Joc, his father Hum, his uncle Skipper and by all those who served the School so well over very many years. The boys dressed for school in a very practical corduroy outfit with shorts and a blue cord jacket over a grey shirt. The best suit or "B" suit was worn at Chapel, on expeditions outside and on special occasions. The staff dressed very informally so were immediately able to go from teaching to active playground duty. We could of course dress more formally to suit the occasion.

The "avant-garde" customs were much admired. As well as attitudes to dress and names, there were other more important reasons for this view. The children performed to remarkable levels at Drama, Music and Art. This could only come about because they weren't being "made" to do everything. The level of questions to a guest speaker or visitor could be very mature and probing. This was because they were not inhibited and they were interested. Although in certain circumstances behavior could get out of control, mostly it did not. They were cheery and welcoming to strangers. This was something they didn't have to be constantly briefed about. Once a colleague told a group of us: "*You can always tell when Rabbits is on dorms when you turn into the Bardwell Road.*" (The corner of Banbury Road and Bardwell Road.)

As the turning in question was two long blocks from the nearest boarding house, this was a comment of affection, not derision. Dorms could be very noisy, but not for long and never out of control. In many other prep schools of the time boys went to dormitories, washed, and brushed their teeth in absolute silence, not even a good night.

2. Science Club in operation, 1962

CHAPTER 3

I Return for Good

I returned to Oxford and the Bardwell Road "for good" in 1970. I served for twenty four years, with a break for a two term sabbatical in the 1980s, and a year's exchange to Australia in the early 1990s.

The new regime had taken time to firmly establish itself. A number of colleagues had retired. The most important task of a headmaster is the appointment of good staff and this the new Headmaster did most successfully. Continuity and stability are so important. Many of those appointed then gave the best years of their life to the School. It takes time to get to know any school and only then are you very valuable to the institution. Keith Ingram, "Inky", the new Head, gradually made his own mark as headmaster.

His predecessor, Joc, as I have already written, was charismatic, a leader and a hard act to follow. This was especially so as Joc had lived his whole life in or near the School and had succeeded his father and uncle. Between the three of them, they had run the School for seventy years.

Joc's successor's humanity and love for children shone above all else. He had some early difficulties. He was appointed internally and had served the School for ten years before taking over as headmaster. Some of his colleagues of the same age and years of service felt that they were entitled to a larger "piece of the action".

Inky was my boss for more than twenty years. I was very fortunate. He cared about one's problems and his advice was invaluable. He was excellent at consulting his staff and at addressing the challenges and problems ahead. Wisely he was vague, deliberately sometimes, about what the future held for us. He was not one to make promises which couldn't be kept. He knew how not to undermine his credibility.

Education generally changed greatly at this time. There had been a revolution of sorts in schools and colleges. Curriculum, discipline, organisation of schools, and the pupil/teacher relationship were all subjected to enormous scrutiny and questioning. We all had to roll with the punches. Actually it wasn't that bad. The school had a liberal outlook. Relations between the adults and children (and that includes adults other than teachers) were healthy. There was none of the distant formal approach to maintaining a school, which meant that life could suddenly become quite challenging.

Parents expected to be consulted even more. Those who took the trouble to come to see us never had a problem. A more organised approach with frequent parent/teacher interviews was not far off. Regular newsletters sent home with reports became ever more informative.

The curriculum, always slowly changing, had to be studied and thoroughly revised. There were increasing demands for timetable time to be found for Science, Art and Carpentry (eventually to become C.D.T. or Crafts, Design and Technology). Music and more practical methods of teaching modern languages became important. We soon had a language laboratory for the practice of spoken French and other modern languages.

Within certain subjects, the wind of change was noticeable. Discipline, which had not previously been a big problem, started to become more difficult. Society was questioning rules and directives. Whereas a couple of whacks with a gym shoe seemed to solve many problems, new approaches for any deliberate insubordination were needed. Giving tasks, or jobs at an inconvenient time, came into favour as a method of punishment. The removal of free time for play was also effective. For harder cases, colleagues made children change into games clothes, report fully changed, and then have to change back. The children didn't like this so they learned to do as they were told.

I suppose that there was some bullying but it was never general or a big problem. The worst case I had to cope with, I came across by accident. I had just returned to School by bicycle when I heard chanting at the edge of the field. I wasn't on duty but I couldn't see who was, and I went along to see what it was all about. A boy, or I assume it must be a boy for I couldn't see him for mud, was standing in the centre of a mob and was being pelted with globs of earth. He was part-American and evidently had angered his playmates.

"Yank, Yank, Yank", they chanted as the mud rained down on him. I walked right up to him, took him by the hand and took him to the nearest building. The tormentors all fled and I can't remember whatever happened to them, if anything.

I took Daniel, the American boy, upstairs and stood him in a bath tub fully clad and washed the mud off him bit by bit. I aroused the ire of the maintenance staff and the cleaning ladies by completely blocking the bath outlet with mud, scouring its surface, covering the floor with thick mud and ruining a bath brush, a sponge and several cloths. At least his eyes, mouth and ears hadn't suffered too much. He cried all the time. I led him next to the changing room which was empty at the time, where he changed into his dry games clothes and then I took him back to his boarding house. I rang his mother, explained that there had been a little local difficulty, and turned the phone over to him.

In later life he became a "G Man", an agent for the F.B.I., so there must be a moral somewhere. I became a friend of his parents and looked out for his two younger brothers when they followed in his footsteps. I had the feeling that Daniel counted the days until he was shot of us four years later, and who could blame him.

The children were not anti-American. We often had American boys and girls at the School for a year or longer, and generally they were very popular. Adam, a member of a leading American family, was head of the house (head boarder prefect). Hougie, a boy from Brooklyn, part of New York City, kept us all amused by his clever use of the Flatbush vernacular. (This local accent is often associated with the very famous *Brooklyn Dodgers* baseball team.)

Though I don't doubt that bullying did occur, most of the children had such respect for the School that many potential bullying incidents were headed off or squashed by the older children.

The boarders in Inky's time were divided into four small houses (no more than twenty) for eight to nine year olds. There were two middle houses (twenty five and fifty) for ten to eleven year olds, and two senior houses (forty and eighty) for twelve to thirteen year olds. Some day boys came to board for their final year with us in order to get ready for their next school if it was a boarding school. With this separation of age groups, the older ones didn't bully the younger ones. Also the class teachers had a good grip on their "forms" and were able to deal with any problems.

The most difficult discipline problem was the large (more than one hundred children) hour-long supervised homework (prep) session. This was held in a dining hall where the tables and chairs were very close together. The secret of success was to arrive early, space the chairs and tables, and allow no one to enter until there was no talking. Then show that you expected every child to be organised. Never sit down. Never take questions or comments. Patrol slowly while standing, and at the finish maintain silence, clear up and organise departure by rows. It had to be a military operation or there would be chaos. One winter we had power cuts caused by miners defying the Government. A prudent matron had bought up many paraffin liquid gas lamps. These were lit before the switch was pulled and prep went on.

One delightful colleague, Eric, unused to these military ways, seemed to thrive on the chaos in this prep. Neighbours walked their dogs in that direction to see the show through the glass fronted double doors on evenings when Eric was on duty. He couldn't keep order at all anywhere, but he was a thoroughly nice person.

I was in London soon after this winter of the electricity strikes. I went to a Norwegian travel agent to try to organise a cross-country skiing holiday. "No", I was told, "everything is booked for this year." I left my address, giving the address of the School. The agent immediately asked if I knew Eric. She talked about him with great affection. He had successfully tutored her sons and she said that it had made all the difference to their understanding, and that he had highly motivated them. Almost as she talked, she dialled a friend in Norway, spoke a few sentences in Norwegian, and as I was about to leave she told me that my holiday was all arranged. I simply had to get to Newcastle in two weeks time, catch the *S.S. Leda* for Bergan, and all would be well. It was. It only goes to show that we should not write people off for apparent failure. I am sure Eric was far better at private tutoring than I could ever have hoped to be.

There were others with unusual gifts. When the children first came to the School, they entered something called the "E block", which was a separate unit for those making the transition into the School, for their lessons. It was a special part of the School seldom visited by the rest of us. Some children were boarders, sent away at the age of eight. Life could have been hell for them, but it wasn't.

Ann was an institution. Her purse was always stocked with Smarties and other goodies. The boys and girls quickly settled down to work with her without realising that they were actually working and achieving.

Ruth took another class. She had strong views on many subjects, but she kept these to herself among the very young. She was the "saint" who gathered up all the lost property at the end of term and tried to return it to whom it belonged. Once, so overwhelmed with exhaustion, she delivered the lost items for number two on her list to location three, and for number three to location four until I pointed this out. We then went back with a cart and moved it to the right place. When I first arrived at the School, my digs had fallen through, and she insisted I come home with her. She put me up in her dining room for a week until a more permanent home could be found.

Longers, always in a rush, and seemingly disorganised,

looked after the clever ones during their first year. No one was ever quite clear what he did with them, but they obviously worked happily. Once it was decided to replace him and to install someone in his place who could get a great deal more accomplished with these gifted children. Soon there were complaints from parents about stressed-out children and Longers was returned to his familiar role.

The Major was always available. He told the smaller ones stories about his past exploits. These stories were exaggerated when retold by his colleagues to make it seem that he had and could solve most of the problems of the world. He spent considerable time telling the children to stand up straight, and to take their hands out of their pockets. They loved his apparent militaristic approach, and I noted with interest when they returned years later to look in at the School, they always asked after the Major. His too was an influence which made them feel at home during their first year.

Rabbits largely operated further up the School, teaching History, English and Latin and producing plays as well as running a house. He really came into his own when snow fell. We never did have a repeat of the long freeze previously described, but sometimes snow fell in large quantities with no warning. Among his many responsibilities was "The Master in Charge of Snow." Backed firmly by the Headmaster, he had wide powers to requisition practically anything and anyone to lay on an instant winter program of events. All maintenance work stopped, much to the irritation of the Bursar, and ropes, benches, posts and signs were placed at strategic locations. Younger staff, who might have thought that they had the afternoon off if their game had not been due to play, would suddenly find themselves on the river bank, behind an ancient umbrella, staving off a snowball attack by fifty children. Other areas saw the building and judging of snowmen and sculptures.

I was ordered onto my Norwegian cross-country skis and told to glide around the fields. This would stir the little men into an additional frenzy of snowballing. Supervised slides were built with bales of straw alongside to prevent heads hitting the walls.

Through it all, the Master in Charge of Snow, clipboard in hand, and with the help of a noisy whistle, directed traffic and activities, with the Headmaster hovering discreetly nearby to make sure that no one could just disappear off the scene without being noticed. When it occurred, this was an incredible performance and transformed a dreary afternoon into one which combined exercise and fun.

Two years after my return, Inky made a very positive move. His deputy, Guv, was involved with the running of many parts of the School. He ran a boarding house, organised games groups, looked after the common room, and drew up and amended the timetable, as well as teaching fifteen periods a week. Inky decided to make him joint headmaster. Inky was still more senior than Guv so it might not have looked very significant. The following diagram demonstrates how the School should have ideally operated.

CHILDREN

↑

STAFF   ←   HEADMASTER   ←   PARENTS

↑

GOVERNORS

However, times were changing and there were increasing demands on the headmaster's time from outside the School. I.A.P.S. work (Incorporated Association of Preparatory Schools) included sports committees, serving on the Council of IAPS, visits and consultation with senior schools, curriculum development, organised parent activities, studies and consultation regarding future development, appeals for money, and governors and subcommittee meetings. Both Headmasters taught classes, did their corrections, and ran some school activities as well as being aware of how each child progressed. By making Guv joint headmaster, he was eligible to represent the School with these outside commitments on an equal basis. In this way, both were able to continue to be active and up-to-date within the School and the School was properly represented externally.

The School ran well and parents were impressed. Inky and Guv had key people running parts of the School, and as they were both so active in the day-to-day teaching, activities, games, and even the odd duty, they were in touch with what was happening. They met once a week to ensure coordination and to deal with any problems. Because the School ran well there was good morale among the staff and this communicated itself to the children.

The Dragon School remained a leader among schools. The atmosphere was excellent and there was a very close understanding and rapport amongst everyone. The boys and girls were much admired. The respect children had for each other was the strongest feature of the School and many people wanted to discover how it worked.

To enroll a child, the parents simply had to register them, preferably at birth. There was no entrance exam so all registrations were welcome. Despite being considered the best prep school in the country, it had a non-selective entrance. Those parents who didn't move quickly were likely to find their child on a waiting list, and he or she might never get to the School.

One set of parents I came to know well drove their car along the Bardwell Road and parked as near to the School entrance as possible, at a time just prior to the exit from lessons for the day. They then gently lowered the windows and waited. Of course they were ignored as the ebb and flow of children and staff passed them. They had done the same at other schools and they told me that it was obvious to them why they wanted their son to come to our School. The atmosphere was electric and there was a sense of purpose. Everyone seemed to be in a hurry to get to tea and then back to the playground to play or to the field for some kind of activity. Later when they were guided by a ten year old boy to the Headmaster's study, they were assured by their guide that he too would be enrolling his children at the Dragon School at some future date.

The job of Registrar was thought to be part-time but increasingly the demands expanded. Some evidence that the child could read and write by the time they came to us, was asked for.

We recognised dyslexia as a problem and we had teachers trained to give lessons to correct it. The Registrar wanted any information about such problems.

There had always been a master in charge of day boys and girls. Given the size of the School, and the fact that the headmaster played a full part in the life of the School, this was inevitable. In time, a senior master was appointed who took on the timetable, the organising of the stooges, and dealing with staff absences. Staff had to attend meetings and conferences connected with their subjects, their other responsibilities, and games. One strong feature of the School was that many of us were specialist teachers yet we taught at least one discipline far removed from our own. The senior Music master taught a class of Mathematics and I taught English, though I was primarily a Mathematics and Science person. Quite apart from making us more rounded teachers, we were more likely to appreciate the problems in areas of the School other than our own.

The "reputation" of the School in another way depended on the quality and number of scholarships received by the children to attend public schools (senior independent secondary schools). Parents expected proper preparation for scholarships. A full scholarship could be worth £60,000 (in 1990 economic terms) over five years. Many parents couldn't afford that level of fees, and if they were to provide the best education for a clever child, it had to be via a scholarship.

I was never closely involved with this part of the School effort. I did tutor a number of children for Science exams, but until the 1980s this subject wasn't taken seriously. Results in the Classics, English, Mathematics, French and the General Paper largely determined the winners. The preparation was carefully orchestrated. Streaming by ability for the Classics (Latin and Greek), English, Mathematics and French were crucial. The syllabi for the top sets from the age of ten were fairly demanding. Greek was only taught to the top sets.

The demands of the various schools could be very different. They did not issue a syllabus so one was dependant on previous exam papers from that school. There was no common scholarship exam or anything like it. The experts were against this happening as it might erode their competitive advantage. I well remember that in Mathematics, one school demanded a fairly good understanding of probability. No other schools required this, so if one's candidates were thoroughly prepared in this, then there was an advantage, especially as many prep schools might not even realise that it was a requirement.

I used to help Chris, the senior Mathematics master, in small ways. When the candidates were in the final year of preparation, he would set work for the holidays, and in particular, for the four week break near Easter. The exams took place in May in stages, so a boy or girl could try for two different schools: most tried only once. Chris had children answering questions from previous papers, and these were sent to him for correction, or he might visit their home. He had some high-powered friends to help with solutions where required. This all ended with a "reading party" at School for the last three days of the break where work was reviewed in many subjects.

This preparation for the sitting of the exams was also carefully thought out. Mock interviews for the candidates took place and sometimes I helped with this. They had to learn to sit up, look the questioner in the eye, and not to give false answers. It was no use saying you favoured a certain author unless you had read several of his books. They also had to be positive and to speak clearly and to show some sense of humour. They shouldn't be shy about their accomplishments, especially in non-academic areas.

Detailed preparation before and during the exam could be important. The exams were nearly always written at the public school. I went with Chris once to a local school where the exams were to be taken in the "Old Geography Room". This room was seldom used so it was in need of a thorough cleaning. Chris arranged for a window catch to be unlocked. We drove to a location nearby one Sunday evening, taking a bucket, mop, sponges, cloths, broom and deodorant. We set about cleaning the room very thoroughly and opened the windows to allow fresh air to circulate. Fortunately the teaching area was empty on Sunday evening, so our cleaning didn't attract attention. We left trying not to leave footprints anywhere. The point was that in previous years some candidates developed runny noses and even had attacks of asthma. The School was indifferent so we had to do something about it.

With another school, forty miles away, Chris showed another kind of expertise. It was a large school and over the years Chris had learned the layout of the classrooms. In order not to disrupt the School routine, the exams were held in a variety of locations, often far apart one from each other. At times, the candidates had to move swiftly from one location to another so as not to miss the start of the next exam. One year Chris was paid the ultimate compliment. An internal candidate, a boy already at the public school, followed Chris and the others, as the arrangements were so tricky that he felt that, although he had been at the School for many months, he still might lose his way.

Chris organised for the boys to stay with friendly house-masters. He had a bag with drink, kleenex, sweets and tennis balls and he knew where it was safe to let off steam between sessions. Although these schools did to some extent look after the candidates and feed them, they needed someone to talk to and to organise them between sessions. There were even two mornings when Chris took the boys to a morning of exams, drove the forty miles to the Bardwell Road, taught two periods, and drove back in time to collect them and to take them to lunch.

The exams lasted four days and often candidates had to hang around at the end. The earlier papers had, by then, been corrected and examiners would summon certain candidates to question them verbally regarding some of their answers.

Over the years the public schools, increasingly eager to attract the best candidates, offered special awards for Art, Music, general ability (including non-academic fields such as sport), and for computing. Most awards only gave partial relief from full fees, so the winning of the major scholarships attracted more and more competition as fees skyrocketed.

Once Mary, the Art mistress, was very concerned about a candidate's portfolio. A selection of the best work had to be taken to be examined. The boy was a boarder, his parents were away, and their house was closed. We had to contact the cleaning lady, drive fifty miles to the boy's home and then start searching. The candidate vaguely remembered his mother moving the paintings, but he had no idea to where. Finally we found them in layers of paper under the carpets in a back room.

The rest of the children wrote entry exams for the school of their choice in their final years. These were set by an independent board, based on an agreed syllabus, and known as *Common Entrance*. Again much special preparation took place.

Many girls took their *Common Entrance* or special entry exams earlier in the year. I used to prepare them as best I could in Mathematics. For some special exams, no previous papers were available, and there was no syllabus. All question papers were carefully collected by the invigilator. Therefore questioning the girls carefully about which questions were asked was a crucial part of the preparation for the next year.

CHAPTER 4

Teaching Science, Mathematics and Beyond

Towards the end of the 1960s, an experimental building was built by a firm where one of the school governors was a director. It contained two classrooms and three large laboratories with a special room for storage and Science preparation. This building, built to a new design, and with new materials, was sold to the School for £1 on the understanding that the firm that built it could inspect the building from time to time to see how it worked out. The walls and roof were substantially built, but internally, shall we say, better materials could have been used for ceilings and doors. The laboratories were well laid out with tables for individual experiments by each member of a class of twenty four. The whole class could sit on stools by a large demonstration bench in each lab. Reptiles and animals, if they escaped from the biology laboratory upstairs, could freely circulate through the building. Fortunately they headed for the warmer parts of the building so we knew where they might be found. A snake, coming out of a cupboard unexpectedly, could, and did, take part in a Physics lesson downstairs.

We gradually built up equipment to teach Physics, Chemistry and Biology. The children in their last three years had the chance to do experimental work most weeks. We used a syllabus adapted from the Nuffield Science courses which had been adopted by the I.A.P.S. As water, gas and electricity were laid on we could do nearly all the practical work in the syllabus.

Science came to be accepted as part of the overall program of work and Science Club declined. The demands of the practical work preparation and the full teaching and duty requirements were too much. To run the Club successfully required someone available most of the time.

Upstairs were the two new classrooms. Downstairs were the Chemistry and Physics classrooms. We had no fume cupboard for Chemistry so demonstrations could be interpreted as gas attacks upstairs. The Thermit Reaction, where a long magnesium fuse lit a mixture so as to produce iron which would flow (in theory) into a crack in a piece of cast iron, was a favourite. I made the mistake (only once) of allowing a class to heat sodium on a piece of crucible held by tongs over a Bunsen flame. Despite warnings, one boy placed the burning mixture in a sink. Sodium reacts violently with water and more so when hot. There was a mighty explosion which cleared the lab. Thereafter, this was done as a demonstration behind multi-layers of plexiglass. We did use protective goggles and we did have a first aid kit, and in particular we were in a position to deal with eye problems very quickly.

Cooperation and group teaching are very important. As the Science staff increased, each one of us would be responsible for arranging the practical details of each part of the syllabus. Each week we met for forty minutes and explained to the others, demonstrating with equipment where necessary, exactly what was involved for the next practical lesson. We also had to provide notes as well as any reference notes and books, and indicate which chapters of texts which might be useful. We eventually were able to employ a full time laboratory technician and this helped with repairs and renovations. It also so meant that a wider range of experimental work could be covered.

In Mathematics the team approach was crucial. The syllabus was adapted to include new topics like the binary system and sets and Venn diagrams. We received in-service training from a member of staff with a Mathematics degree. Nearly all teachers had degrees but not necessarily in a discipline which had much to do with their teaching.

The important factor was one's ability as a teacher, and an understanding of children and how they learnt. Good teachers could teach a wide range of disciplines, but even for the most experienced a thorough preparation of lessons was most important.

The Mathematics syllabus was largely dictated by the requirements of the various examinations for entry to the next school. All sets within an age group were organised by ability, and adjacent sets tried to follow similar syllabi. The order of topics was up to us, but we did have common tests across two or three sets every so often to keep us working together. There were never sets of text books which covered anything but a small part of any syllabus. The syllabus was always under review and constantly changing. One had a wide range of notes, sets of examples, problems and overhead transparencies.

Mental arithmetic was considered essential. We tried to make it fun by mixing up tables with such things as, "Multiply by the number of fingers on your two hands and subtract the feet of a centipede, before writing your answer."

Jonathan and two brothers, James and Philip, were very good at this and on occasion I would ask them to make up a sequence of Mathematics operations.

There were amusing moments. I used stick men and animals

in connection with Algebra problems. I even allowed colours to liven up the diagrams.

"Six milk maids milk enough cows in two hours to produce milk for the farm. How long would four milk maids take to perform the same task milking at the same rate?"

One of my best students went on to her next school, a strict old-fashioned girls' boarding school. She was soon carpeted in front of the Headmistress to explain this flippant approach. Her mother, not at all impressed with the Headmistress, passed on this gem.

Another boy, arriving at his public school, went into a class in Mathematics, and spying the overhead projector, exclaimed aloud that it was a "Beverley Machine". Unfortunately and unknown to him the new Mathematics master was called Mr. Beverley and the boy was firmly reprimanded and paraded in front of the Headmaster. The Head knew me well and was in fact the parent who parked his car at the School when choosing a prep school for his own son. He handled it all very diplomatically. To go to another school where the approach was distant, formal and strict, was difficult.

To provide variety to my teaching of Mathematics and Science, I taught Geography. This I much enjoyed, particularly as the syllabus was flexible. I was able to do work with Forestry, Mineral Extraction, Farming (mostly wheat growing and fishing) and Transportation (rail, road and the seaway) in Canada. It made me seek Canadian sources of teaching materials (mostly slides and booklets) and I made some of my teaching films on site which included the trains, both freight and passenger, and the St. Lawrence Seaway. There was copper ore, mined and smelted in the

Gaspé region of Quebec, and fishing of lobsters off Prince Edward Island. I visited and filmed logging in the forest of Northern Ontario and grain elevators in Alberta. I covered the Rocky Mountains, hydroelectric dams, and Niagara Falls.

This, combined with local British Geography and our expeditions, I found very interesting. I started to think of taking on a form for teaching. I had two periods a week of thirty five minutes for Geography and three periods for Science. For Science, we did the Bunsen Burner, its history and use, purifying rock salt, some chromatography, examining of all sorts of materials, weighing and measuring blocks of solids, and we each made a microbalance. One term we did Biology. Evidently I couldn't provide the expertise for examining live locusts and gerbils, hatching eggs or the study of the body parts of dead rats.

I decided to take on English. This was risky as I couldn't write, spell, or use grammar and punctuation properly. We had to teach handwriting so I had to totally change my own. I felt I needed at least eight teaching periods a week in order to get to know the class of children. They were children streamed to the bottom form of five or six groups of the C block (aged ten to eleven). It was quite a challenge, both teaching them and handling the subject. The taker of every form had the responsibility of looking after the children in many ways. They could be fractious and niggly with each other. Somehow we had to get on. It was important to instill a sense of purpose into what we did, but also to insist on proper behavior both in the form room and elsewhere. What rules there were had to be enforced. These included valuing one's own property and that of others, making an effort to do homework as required, and to hand it in on time. There was a big effort each year to look after the room, to not break anything, to organise the desks so that books and writing things could be found. Working closely with these children and writing fully about them on reports kept everyone in touch. If a parent really wanted to know what was going on with their child they came to see the form teacher.

Children in the bottom form had problems. It could be lack of motivation, frustration from dyslexia, or inability to get on with others. The plays which I have described elsewhere were very important, especially for morale.

The form competed as a unit in two sports, in athletics at the end of the year and for swimming (the School had a large well-maintained heated outdoor swimming pool). Athletically I am afraid that social class made a big difference. The more academically competent children were also better athletes than we were. We almost always finished last. The swimming was different. There were teams of four and the whole School was involved. Here the boats (the name given to these teams of four) could win the division in which case they were promoted to a higher division the next time there were swimming relays. The bottom team was dropped to the next lower division. I never made any boy or girl swim but those who had passed their swimming tests always wanted to have a "go".

We followed a syllabus with story writing, poetry and reading. I usually had a colleague to help with the reading which was important, both for understanding and for verbal skills. In the summer term we had an outside examiner come for the English Speaking Board tests. These were in three parts: a poem recited from memory, a reading from a book chosen by the child (with the particular passage selected by the examiner) and then each child gave a "talk" on a subject of their choosing. This could be illustrated with slides, maps, and overhead transparencies. The children put a great deal of effort into this activity. Sailing, Holidays and Golf were favourite topics.

I suggested to David that he obtain a scorecard from his home golf course and a variety of golf clubs. A chauffeur appeared with the clubs in a bag but no scorecard. I should have known better. David's father, who was very wealthy, owned the golf course and as only family played, there was no need for a card. Probably the lowest point came one dreary winter month. The form and I were not getting on, paying much attention to anything and nothing was accomplished. I was really fed up. I arrived at the classroom and I just occupied myself by cleaning the floor by the radiators. It was a few minutes before the children realised that I was "on strike". Amazingly they all found something to do, reading or writing or working in a workbook. We had a quiet and productive half hour. Nothing was said.

It was not all a success by any means. Some parents felt their children were not accomplishing anything so they removed them from the School, but we did care and we did try. As several children made it to good universities such as Oxford, I assume their problems were sorted out somewhere later. I would like to think that some of them were being well looked after when they were with me.

When politicians and educators talk of rewarding exceptional teachers with merit pay, I firmly disagree. We aren't effective if we teach in tight little units. The team approach was crucial to any success that we had, and if one of us taught well enough to deserve an extra increment, then we all did, and equally.

Also the approach to teaching was becoming fairly "exam directed" and in danger of becoming relentless and humourless. We all felt this but we were prisoners of the system. We all welcomed the increasing time given to practical Science, Music and to Craft, Art, Design and Technology.

Colleagues were sometimes away and I had to fill in for them. Once, and only once, I was directed to a lesson for French. I speak the language reasonably well, having been born and brought up in Quebec. On this day they had been told to read and to write about a pamphlet they all had. It was about seals, *"Les Petits Phoques"*. A number of questions came my way. The pamphlet gave a lurid account of "red necks" streaming onto the pack ice in the Gulf of St. Lawrence to brutally club young seals to death as soon as they had been born. On my many visits to this part of Canada I had learned a good deal about seals. I gave a spirited defence explaining that most seal pups were humanely killed to prevent over-population now that many of the natural predators (such as sea lions) were no longer there. I clearly made a mistake as the Headmaster had several phone calls about a member of his staff who had dared to defend the killing of young seals.

Even when filling in for colleagues, there was often an opportunity to do some useful teaching. In the above instance, I put the case for the culling of seals. This was another side to the story which I am sure many children did not realise. My friendship with the fishermen of the Gulf of St Lawrence, whose catches have been decimated by the seal population getting out of control, gave me this opportunity. I thought that I had explained that in the absence of predators of the seals, it was necessary to do a cull. However I noticed that I wasn't asked to take any more French lessons!

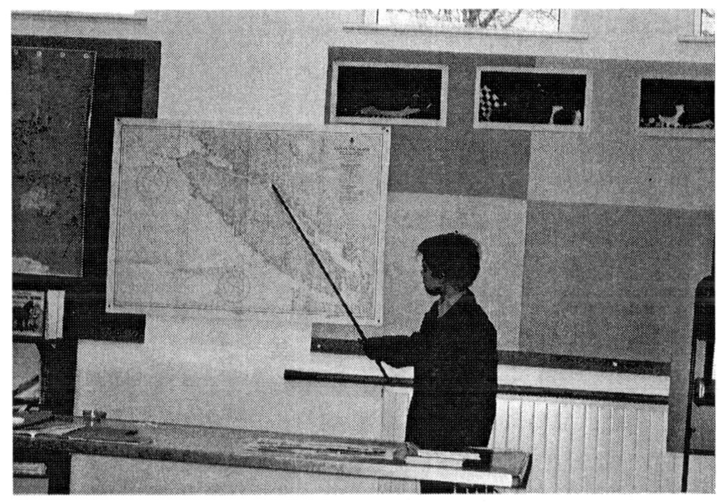

3. Micheal lectures for the English Speaking Board about sailing in British Columbia, early 1990s

4. Felix Astalwor of Middle Five, early 1980s

CHAPTER 5

Games, Visits and Boarders

Games didn't change much for me, except that older groups of children were assigned to me, and sometimes I had up to thirty at a time on my own. These took place for half the children during the hour before lunch on Mondays, Tuesdays, Thursdays and Fridays and in the afternoon on Wednesdays or Saturdays. It was exhausting but rewarding work.

Both Inky and Guv found time to take games. Guv and I shared a Rugger group. Guv ran a Cricket game known as the *"Snapdragons"*. Inky was in charge of a less-gifted section of the same group. They were cricketers who liked playing only occasionally, but were not very proficient and preferred to spend time playing tennis, sculling, or even reading. They played once a week and also played similar teams in other schools.

Kosak was one of them. His father came to Oxford University when Kosak was ten. He spent a very happy year with us, but when the time came, he had to return to Japan. Kosak was determined to return when he was thirteen when his mates were in their last term. By leaning on his grandmother (for funds) and local friends for lodging, he returned. He had invested in the latest and smartest cricket gear. As he hadn't played for two years, he was placed with the *"Snapdragons"*. He was strong and demolished the opposition batting. He was quickly sent to a school game where he hit the ball hard but was also out easily. The point of the story is not only that the Headmaster took a game on a regular basis, but the bonds formed by outsiders who spent a year with us were very strong. There was something about the atmosphere of camaraderie which was infectious. There were many Kosaks who loved to return if they could manage it.

Charles came to board with us from France for the Easter term. Very polite and obviously bright. He kept very much to himself, certainly with all adults.

Towards the end of the following June, I was surprised to learn he was with us again. Evidently, his friends in the school had convinced him that he should return to school for the end of the school year.

He did open up. He told me that in France he was well taught by good conscientious teachers, but at the end of the day, the children went one way and the teachers the other. There was almost no contact outside lessons. He was mature enough to appreciate that the excellent rapport we had at the Dragon School between adults and children was a very significant factor in what the school was all about. He recognised the unique rapport made it possible to do many worthwhile things at school in a way which he said was not possible in France.

Taking a team away could be an adventure. Once, at short notice, I had to take a rugby fifteen to play another school. The match was due to kick off at 2.30pm. We were late due to heavy traffic and didn't arrive until 2.05pm, twenty minutes late. The referee and home team were already on the field. The ball was teed up ready for the kick off. The referee asked me to get the team on the field as he wanted to start at 2.15pm instead of the agreed 2.30pm. This would mean our team running straight onto the fields from changing to kick off. Any team needs a warm up, not only to get rid of the cramp of a bus trip, but to get ready to play. I told them to go to the far end of the field and to form a huddle leaning inwards as in American football. This would attract the referee. Then they were to break up and do warm up exercises, standing well apart. The referee was not pleased and took up more time by coming to tell me so. In the end, we didn't start early and we defeated our opponents who hadn't lost a game that season.

Games, or sport, are an important part of every child's education. Too many children are discouraged from taking part in games. Some are put off team sport for life by unsympathetic treatment or an early traumatic experience. I will never claim to have been at all gifted at taking games. In this instance however I felt that the referee, clearly having a pressing engagement after the match, could have caused our players much distress. It wasn't right for him to expect the boys to step straight from the bus onto the field against a home side which had had plenty of time to warm up in preparation for the match.

One also wants to avoid situations where players are under particular pressure from the coach to perform. Individual tension is a bad thing. In the team situation this is different because a team playing well together will perform better than the individuals who make up the team. Similarly a team with talented players, who don't perform as a unit, can be very unsuccessful. The changing facilities must also be good. If they are too crowded, clothes and valuables can lost, or if the shower and toilet facilities are inadequate, this may affect the children's enthusiasm. I felt that some of the children who tried to be often "off games" had a fear and loathing of the changing facilities. I did enjoy the rare occasion when I was asked to take a team away.

During the summer term, in the evenings, I started some baseball. I had a glove, a bat and a few baseballs with me. It started with just throwing the ball about. Several boys and at least one girl had acquired gloves on foreign visits or if the family had been in a baseball playing country. Beirut (with its American University) and Taiwan were two such locations. The game needs a backstop, and despite using the back side of a tennis fence, foul balls rained off bats and one time hit a tennis player on his back. We had to move. The ground staff created a baseball diamond for us with a back netting of our own. Each year I added to the equipment, including kneepads, chest protector and mask for a catcher. Absolutely anyone could turn up to play, and in time there were too many. We had to organise into teams and play a league schedule. The children predictably chose the *Mets, Yankees, Giants, Red Sox, Dodgers and Blue Jays*.

We added bases and not just loose sacks to our equipment, a pitcher's mound and a proper home plate. I quickly demonstrated some basic rules before each evening play. There was always a nucleus of boys who had previously, in a baseball playing area, played Little League Baseball.

We managed to play some games with other schools. We played the American School from London and Appleby College from Oakville, Ontario. Over the years we won as often as we lost. Finding pitchers with reasonable control was the key. Appleby College came over on a choir or cricket tour most years, but fitted us in somehow. Nearly eighty youngsters played at least once a week.

The baseball was a small part of the evening sports time. The main school sport, cricket, was treated like any other. It was voluntary and there were usually enough for two spontaneous, informal cricket games to take place. Athletics took place around the edges, mainly the field events. There was swimming training in the pool and life saving, kayaking and canoeing in the Cherwell River at the bottom of the fields. A full program of tennis was in operation, and on some courts coaching was available. There was even a climbing wall. It was well-organised and must have given an enormously good impression for any visitor happening along the Bardwell Road looking over the picket fence out on the fields.

On Wednesday mornings there were optional activities for an hour for all those in their last two years. This freed the play-ground for the younger children who, on other days, took current affairs. The guest speakers kept coming. Two Canadian High Commissioners, two Shadow Ministers from Parliament, one Mayor of Oxford, the manager of Oxford United football team, a senior cricket correspondent, and a director of the Hudson Bay Company. Rarely were we refused. I asked one of the Canadian High Commissioners, who had been a senior Minister in many Canadian Governments, why he had come. In nearly five years at the High Commission, we were the first and only school to invite him, so he told me.

Every second year we went to Westminster and in between, the law courts, the Guildhall, the Bank of England, Lloyds Insurance, the Baltic and Tea Exchanges or to the Stock Market.

At Westminster, we had a tour of all the public areas including the Robing Room, St. Stephen's Hall, the Lords and Commons and Westminster Hall. Our guide was a clerk attached to the Commons to whom we paid cash for the tour. Our local Member was a Government Minister and I accused him, as he organised these tours, of supporting the black economy. He was very amused once when we arrived as all the boys and girls gained entry but I failed to get past the metal detector.

In the afternoon we tried to get to the Prime Minister's questions. This wasn't easy as each M.P. can only request two tickets for this and only once every two weeks. There are so many requests that often they go to a ballot.

There were many notable visits including one where our high profile M.P. host had the heavy-weight champion of the world, George Foreman, in tow as well as us. Foreman was very smartly dressed. I insisted our children had freshly shone shoes and a handkerchief peeking out of the suit breast pocket. Even then Mr Foreman seemed to be so much better dressed than we were for this big occasion.

Once, having enough tickets, we were seated in the narrow rows directly above the Members of the House of Commons and not in the larger visitors' gallery at the end. Some boys faced me on the other side. The Prime Minister, Mrs. Thatcher, had a cold, could hardly be heard, and no one wanted to take advantage of her! One of our boys, who thought he knew it all, settled even lower in his seat, looked bored and as if he was nodding off. At that point there was a sudden and violent outburst. Most of the Members had left, including the Prime Minister. The out-burst continued with shouting and some very unparliamentary language. The Speaker, unable to calm the shouting down, suspended the sitting. The boy opposite sat bolt upright and got up as if to flee but the Commons guard made him sit down. Later I asked him what he thought of it all. "It wasn't at all like you said it would be", he replied.

If we couldn't get into the Commons I usually had tickets to the Lords. These were more easily obtained, as it was thought that, by comparison, the Lords would be dull. Just before going there I met the noble Lady who had provided the tickets. She had been a School Governor and was currently a Minister of State at the Foreign Office. I had foolishly asked her if anything worthwhile was likely to happen.

Well, she immediately went into action once the Lord Chancellor was firmly on the woolsack. There were Foreign Office questions that day. One noble Lord was told that he had just scored an own goal. Those Lords accustomed to nodding off early in the session following a good lunch, were soon on their feet competing for the Lord Chancellor's attention after a most lively session when one Lord, a former party leader, wondered out loud what was going on. The Minister then rose and left. She looked pointedly up at me in the visitors' gallery as if to say, "Well did that make the grade, was that what you expected?" I had been firmly put in my place.

The remaining thirty or more activities depended on the interests of the staff and children. The Agriculture class visited a series of friendly farms just outside the city limits. In those days most could be reached in fifteen minutes or less. Lambs born one week could be visited later to see how they were getting on. There was a Bridge group (taken by three staff members), including Guv and Ann of the E block. Mahjongg, brass rubbings, shooting (with rifles in the School range) and Oxford tours. There was an Oxford Panorama group that studied the city as if they were all town planners. They drew maps, made models and even made presentations and suggestions to the City Council about planned city developments.

For the younger children, with the requirements of external examiners still years away, there were special visits during class time. I took a group once to a nearby airbase for a firefighting display. The fires in the old equipment, sprayed with petrol, were impressive and the fire fighters worked away with hand-held extinguishers. Unfortunately the fire looked like spreading to a nearby hanger so a huge truck with masses of foam was summoned. That was even more impressive.

All of these activities were bound to have a great influence on the children and I was always grateful to the School for encouraging us to make full use of all the opportunities offered.

During the 1960s the boarders spent most weekends of the term at School. Even half terms only came into the program of events gradually. The weekends were important for the boarders, as they needed to learn to get on with each other, to relax, to have fun at school and to profit by taking part in some of the activities offered.

During the 1970s, the road network in the south of England greatly improved. It was now possible for parents of boarders to come to see their sons every weekend (girls only started to board in the 1990s). Some children, particularly if they were from broken homes with parents competing for their affections, became very dependent on the weekend visits. It was an ongoing problem to explain to parents that they needed some weekend time with other children of their age.

I was Housemaster of Gunga Din (of Rudyard Kipling's books) for five years. I continued to be very busy in the School in every way while I was Housemaster. I was very dependent on two tutors to help me. Up to the early 1970s the form master was the key pastoral figure. Though the School was over five hundred in number, the form master taught his or her class at least once a day and knew the children well. With the increase in specialised teaching this became more difficult, so tutors largely took over. I had forty five in the house, they were all twelve or thirteen year olds so we each took one third.

I discovered that having a good matron was terribly important. I once had a bad matron, who rode off one night on her motorbike with all my good silver, never to be seen again. Otherwise I was very lucky. Some of them were comparatively young and I think there was some criticism of this.

Annie was such a matron. She was a formidable presence when she wanted to be. Otherwise she was a "ball of fire", and always was helping and arranging activities, and games and entertainments for the children. Because she was young (less than twenty) she was very much on the same wavelength as these children who had recently become teenagers. The matrons had a very good rapport with the boys. Not only did they look after them from morning until night, they were also an important link to the parents. They were especially good at special events, birthday teas, and looking after the boys' "tuck". Once I had to duck for apples in a large tub at Halloween. It took many attempts. It wasn't good for one's sinus!

Fire prevention was paramount. The boarding house was an old building and we were confined to the top two floors. The Common Room occupied the ground floor. There was a step ladder and a dimly lit corridor and one climbed this to reach a key, which when turned, set off the fire alarm. This was all very well, but I wondered if the button behind the glass plate and in everyone's view in the Common Room, would work. One day two of us tried to remove the glass plate. It broke. We pressed the button. Nothing happened. The Bursar was hopping mad and tried to send me a bill for its repair. I replied that if we had to depend on that bell we would have all been burned alive.

There was always a boy who acted as fire officer. In the event of adults being unable to help, he was trained in how to check if the house was empty and make sure that everyone was accounted for. The tutors helped me by taking dormitory duty one night a week. One night, the fire bells throughout the School had been extensively tested all day, and a tutor, coming downstairs for a moment, heard the fire bell and thought nothing of it. Ten minutes later, he was deep in conversation, when there was a knock on the door. It was the boy fire officer, in pyjamas and dressing gown. With his clipboard in hand he said all were present and correct and please could the tutor come into the playground where the boys and matrons were getting cold and give permission to return to the house? This was the first he knew about it! The system had worked. Sometime later I had fire drills at 3.00am. Two dormitories slept on. New louder bells had to be installed. The Bursar was not amused.

I used to take complaints about boys from staff very seriously and follow them up. I would ask for reports about better behavior and cooperation. The reports soon died away to a trickle, I think most of them could have been sorted out by the staff concerned.

After the School service on Sunday morning parents would come to coffee. One boy's parents had won the Irish sweepstakes and sent him to our School with the winnings. The father was a city street cleaner and didn't think he belonged with the other parents.

I would go down to a lamppost outside to talk to them while the tutors and matrons carried on with the coffee.

Not that there was any lack of things going wrong. David, desperate to make the School hockey team, did not own up to feeling ill. In the middle of the night, I was awakened and asked to come quickly. David could hardly breathe. A phone call brought the School nurse in a hurry. An ambulance came immediately and took David to the hospital. A week later he was back, hopefully the wiser. He still made the team.

The clever little devils figured out that there was no duty person near the swimming pool at certain lunch breaks. During this time a local girls' school had the use of the pool. The lady supervising the girls was often late and easily distracted. The boys and girls met beside the pool, which had a high retaining wall around it, for some unsupervised activities! We had a cafeteria for meals, so no one checked when the boys had lunch. A suspicious lady teacher suspected something was going on, but they managed to elude her.

Then the craftier ones leaned on a day boy whose father owned a local restaurant. He arranged for them to have a meeting in an upstairs room in the restaurant where there were cubicles. Various bogus requests came in for the children concerned to have Saturday lunch with their parents.

Eventually a note from one to another was dropped by accident in the road. It simply said Gunga Din. I read it and all was revealed. I went to the Headmistress of the girls' school and she soon had the girls performing tasks in an attic on weekends. I apologised to the owner of the restaurant whom I knew well. He said that the boys had told him that they had my permission to be there. Inky was not at all impressed and especially the fact that I hadn't noticed all this sooner. He told me that nothing should be done to the boys. "They should be encouraged to lunch with their parents and get to know them better". I don't quite know what he meant but I kept quiet and it worked.

Inky had a way with children and he was loved and very much respected by them. He obviously wanted this whole affair to end right there. He saw no point in any sanctions being imposed. The embarrassment of the exposé had been punishment enough. He was a very wise Headmaster. He would certainly tell us off and rebuke individual children, but there were never sanctions taken against individuals in public in any way.

At morning assembly he would comment about bad behaviour or practice he didn't like and that he wasn't going to tolerate. This carried weight with the community because he never singled out individuals for condemnation at this most public of forums.

We allowed the boarding children to go into town during free time. They went in groups having previously signed out. They were allowed to make purchases as agreed (no sweets) from their pocket money. They dressed casually so that they would blend with the general population. Otherwise there were teenage thugs who would rob them and beat them up. This all took time to organise so that there would be no incidents.

The freedom also allowed the children to climb trees (provided the trees wouldn't suffer) and to have pen knives. Only by having freedoms and learning to use them properly could a child learn to handle them. This was an important part of the School's philosophy.

Some of the older children could become arrogant and forget that other schools and institutions had stricter guidelines. This was certainly true in the case of the Beverley Machine. The freedom which we gave them could be misinterpreted. Once George, a boy who had just left the School, came to see me. He told me that at his public school those boys who were from our School were told they would be watched closely and stamped on if they did not strictly observe the disciplinary code at their present school.

I was upset because no one had misbehaved as far as I knew and it was unfair to single out one group of children in this way. I complained to the boys' school and was delighted to hear that the member of staff who had been behaving in this way had been replaced from his duties of indoctrinating the new boys. The important briefing was now in the hands of the Headmaster. I felt that the temperature would be lowered and everything for George would be handled fairly.

There was a school tuck shop. This was open at set times during the week. One master was in charge. There were girl and boy helpers, and together they went to "Cash and Carry" and discount shops to stack the shelves. A limited selection of sweets, small items and stationery, games and useful items such as key rings were available. In summer there might be a freezer to serve ice creams and lollies (popsicles). The dedicated band of helpers (often from the less able who were not required elsewhere) took their responsibilities very seriously, and it gave them a chance to take part in a business and to learn to handle money. Again this was an important part of what the School stood for.

Children also helped as members of a "Chair Party", which moved furniture around or set it up for special occasions. Again we much depended on the master in charge to organise them and to always be present to supervise and help with this work. They were "paid" in sweets sometimes and with a special supper at the end of term.

Another way in which the boys helped us was connected with letters home at weekends. The boarders all had to send a letter home at least once a week. The small houses were supervised by their housemasters.

For the older boarders those staff on weekend duty supervised the letter writing. At the end of the half hour each boy deposited his letter on an alphabetic pile in the old hall. Letter prefects collected these, sorted them after the School service, and gave me a list. This included the postage - they put on the stamps which was a responsible job as the letters went to many different parts of the world.

For several years before becoming Housemaster I was responsible for the letters. I passed on the names of any boys who had not written. One year a parent, whose family lived in Oxford, returned each Sunday evening to Dublin. He posted all letters there for us at a large saving on price. This arrangement continued for a year with no complaints regarding delivery.

A great deal was done for the children to make their lives more fun and worthwhile. They were certainly made aware of what was done for them and by appealing to their better nature, were always prepared to volunteer to help out. All this was a vital part of making the School function better, and was in everyone's interest.

5. The baseball team waits for the big game with Appleby

CHAPTER 6

Walks and Expeditions

In the late 1960s, staff started taking children for Sunday rambles and walks. To start with they went to a large city park called Shotover which was very overgrown. I was away in Canada at the time, so I did not participate, but soon joined in when I returned in 1970. The children just ran around for an hour playing tag and having fun.

Soon we were using public footpaths and venturing further afield. A group set out with at least a couple of staff and a dozen boys (they were all boarders) and they walked a route agreed with the driver, who would then pick them up three hours later. One driver was once cautioned by the Police for looking at the map as he drove to meet us! One of the attractions was that enough of the best items from the boarder's tea would be kept to one side to be consumed by the walkers on their return. They then went off to see a Sunday film in the school hall.

Two events occurred which helped to popularise this activity. First there was a series of sponsored walks started to make the public aware of the pleasure of walking in the countryside. They were sponsored by local charities connected with the preservation and improvement of the countryside.

The second was the welcoming of parents and friends as part of our walks. Many parents, who wondered where to take their children "out" on a Sunday, preferred to walk with them rather than to go to an expensive restaurant or to make a double trip to and from Oxford to where they lived, which might be as far away as London.

The Countryside Charity Committee organised these walks which took place once a year on a definite route using legal footpaths, some of which hadn't been walked for years. There were check points every two miles, and a beautiful map to show the way. The total distance was about twenty miles and they took us about six hours. Thousands took part and much money was raised.

We arranged our own cars and buses to take us to the start. We numbered at least eighty, but we started late as we couldn't set out until after the School service which didn't finish before 11.00am.

Hoping that the initial check points were not closed, we soon caught up with most of the other walkers. The children could go off in small groups on their own without supervision as the organisation coped. A certain amount of drink was provided and we brought our own packed lunches.

Taking place early in May, the walks led us through countryside at the best time of year. Bluebells carpeted the forests and most trees had just pushed out their first leaves. At the end we had our final check point with a list of names. Transport back to school wouldn't depart without everyone on board. We did however lose a boy on the final half mile once. As he was worth over £1,000 in sponsor money, he was well worth finding! Fortunately, he had found his own lift back to School without coming to our central control.

Then there was the round Oxford walk. Dizzy reconnoitered a thirty three mile route around the city and never more than six miles from the centre. We had to attempt this walk all in one day.

Again it was early May before the planted crops were too high, and while it was relatively cool.

The start was at 5.45am with breakfast at, or close to, School. Walking away from the rising sun across Port Meadow along the river (known as the Isis at Oxford, otherwise the Thames) and up to Cumnor, we then set off across country on a recognised public right of way to our second breakfast. This was a "slap up" affair and for those who had sent their bathers on ahead, a swim as well.

The halt took fifty minutes before we continued east to meet the Isis a second time. Our host, Peter, and his black Labrador, came with us on this section. Soon we were at lunch served by the Major from the back of the School Land Rover, and we had a short school service as well. He trailed us wherever there were road crossings with extra drink and any other supplies. Spare clothing, especially socks by this stage, also helped.

As we now headed north and then west again to Beckley, the pace slackened. Usually the weather cooperated, though the onset of humidity and temperatures in the seventies started to claim a few victims. We never numbered more than twenty so we moved together at a brisk pace. Some years the stinging nettles could be a nuisance to those wearing shorts. At the end of the day we walked south along the River Cherwell, the sun sinking in the west. Everyone had finished or had been rescued by 8.00pm, fourteen hours after the start. Usually a group photo under the School clock at 6.00am was repeated by another fourteen hours later. One father, on a business trip to New York, walked with his son until noon, was collected by a driver, taken to Heathrow Airport, and flew on Concorde arriving in New York about the same time that we finished the walk.

There was a demand for some less high profile walks. The countryside walks continued for a dozen or so years and as a start we used some of the best sections of these routes. Ten mile walks proved very popular with parents who liked to be with their children doing something they all enjoyed which they didn't have to organise themselves. The numbers increased to approximately fifty. We could cope with this number in a hired coach together with the School transport. Certain worthies like Loz, Scotty and Sue were always in close attendance, serving lunch, as well as providing the essential backup over the later stages.

I had to do a thorough reconnaissance of each walk to see that all routes were legal and passable. The timing from start to finish was crucial. A route seeming to take three hours on the map in reality could take twice as long. These visits had to be done close to the time of walking. Once I left three months between the reconnaisance and the walk. A two-mile fence had appeared blocking our route and we had to walk in the rain beside a main road getting wetter as each vehicle sped past.

The Headmaster persuaded the School to invest in a "hot box." Our lunch could then be brought hot to us wherever we had agreed to meet. Once with a large group there was time for Scotty to return to school for a second batch to be eaten further along the route. The total distance of these walks was about ten miles. If we could locate in advance a parent or friend who could provide the venue for tea, so much the better.

Over the years, there were many incidents and not all of them amusing. One walk into the teeth of a gale started well, but as we left our contact with relief by road, the rains came down. Darkness arrived early. Simon, a parent who was a British Airways pilot, always carried flares in his backpack! As the walk ground almost to a halt in the middle of nowhere, thanks to the light provided by the flares, all was revealed. We finished including the last quarter mile up a narrow greasy pathway with morale high.

On another occasion, having checked carefully that our route was legal, I discovered that a farmer had removed the footpath bridge over a deep twelve-foot wide ditch. There was no way around. Happily this omission was noted several days in advance. We made a replacement bridge and installed it the night before as getting it safely in position took some time. I thought it prudent to make a duplicate and hide it in the woods nearby. Sure enough the original was gone when we arrived at the ditch, so the duplicate was put in its place. After a delay we were soon safely across.

The enraged farmer, who no doubt had watched us through his field glasses, was soon bouncing across his fields in his Land Rover toward us. He stayed clear of all adults, found a boy and learned the name of the School. He drove straight to the Bardwell Road and sought out the Headmaster who was in his drawing room having a rest after lunch. He was most forceful and threatening. The Headmaster, not much caring for his manner, threw him out. I never had a complaint or heard directly about the incident ever again.

Only once did we have a serious injury. A boy, playing as he walked with a friend, fell into a small bush. There were shards of glass there and he severed an artery. The blood poured out. Off came our shirts, ripped into narrow strips, as we stopped the flow of blood. We had an adult walker with First Aid training and the School First Aid box on the scene very quickly. Loz, who had been backing us up with drinks, was not far away, and he drove direct to the Hospital Emergency. A friendly farmer phoned ahead so he was expected and he was taken direct to the operating theatre. No long-term harm was done, he was very lucky.

I always had a loathing for walking along roads where there was fast moving traffic. A mystical flat plain known as Otmoor had been little altered since the Middle Ages. It was a great place to walk when it was not too wet. A few cattle wandered about but otherwise there was nobody around. Alas, from time to time, particularly out of season (in winter) it also accommodated a Ministry of Defence firing range. I had been told it was never used for this in Summer, there were too many people about.

A walk was scheduled for the end of the School year. I had done a very thorough reconnaissance but as we approached there were red flags everywhere (indicating Otmoor was out of bounds) and what looked like an S.A.S. Colonel drove down the approach road in front of us. At the last moment we had to follow an un-surveyed ditch around the outside of Otmoor, surrounded by barbed wire entanglements.

The route to the waiting tea on the other side of Otmoor was lengthened. At the end we had to walk along two miles of road - very minor road - but still road. I always did all I could to avoid this kind of road. Sure enough, a mad driver came speeding around a bend and accelerated instead of slowing down. Even though we were strung out in single file along the countryside he managed to force a father carrying his small daughter on his shoulders to leap a road side ditch in a hurry. It was all very unpleasant. Fortunately the injuries were confined to sprains and bruises. The driver however never stopped.

One school year we walked the sixty four mile long Oxfordshire Way in eight equal sections. Seven boys and one girl completed all the sections, and we finished the last mile in a hired steamer from Remenham to Henley in pouring rain. We walked the previous sixty three over nine months. Little did I know it, but this was the best year I had with the walks. The numbers crept up. Increasingly we walked for good causes.

Nicholas and Tim were twin brothers at the School. Both had won scholarships to their next school. Nicholas was killed along with an Irish boy when the Irish Republican Army assassinated Lord Mountbatten, his grandfather.

In his memory, a fund was established to help with "good causes", defined as projects done by graduates of the School which they couldn't afford to support on their own. One I remember was a scientific expedition to Southern Patagonia. Matthew was already in South America and his parents came to join a sponsored walk. This helped him to do all that he planned to accomplish. We also helped Leonard Cheshire V.C., who in retirement founded many Cheshire Homes to help disabled people. From the proceeds of our annual Christmas sale, we donated generously to a Cheshire Home at Oxford for disabled students. Leonard Cheshire raised money for a First World War Memorial Fund. This helped to pay for unexpected disasters anywhere in the world where instant funding was needed.

For the Memorial Fund walk, the reconnaisance was done the previous Easter. It certainly was an epic. We left school at 11.00am on Saturday and we were all back in school and lessons on Monday morning.

The walk took place along the line of the British trenches in Picardy, France, on 1 July 1916. There were 150 walkers. We stayed over Saturday night in a monastery in Arras and at some local hotels.

The advanced preparations were thorough. We were divided into groups of twenty five. Each leader had a map and had been briefed from a video that we made the previous Easter. The advance party organised our lunch and tea. A parent caterer knew just the right amounts of food to buy down to the last baguette. Another parent brought all the tables, chairs and crockery, strapped to a minibus. We then had to check there was enough clearance under a recently built new T.G.V rail line (Le Train à Grande Vitesse is the French high speed train).

It rained hard all the way to France, and overnight, and right up to the start of the walk. It wasn't at all like July 1916 when it was hot and dry. After a brief service at Serre, we set off. Wherever we went there were small cemeteries to the fallen, all well-maintained by the Commonwealth War Graves Commission. We passed through the Newfoundland Park with its splendid Caribou Statue; to Thiepval the Massive Memorial; and on to lunch, French-style by the Lochnagar Crater. The finish was beside a particularly well-sited cemetery in Mametz Wood. Here tea was taken and the heavens opened once more with a vengeance, including thunder and lightning.

The buses sped back to catch the last ferry at Calais (we were a year too soon for the Chunnel). The children had collected all sorts of rusted battlefield souvenirs, most of which had to be left behind because they might damage the bus.

I was always most grateful to the Headmasters for all their support. It must have cost the School some unexpected money to put on these walks. He, together with the Bursar, smoothed the way and when possible, they joined us. As we were in a way reaching out to the community with so many parents and friends involved, I felt the walks helped the School. I was always looking out for possible difficulties and what might go wrong. In fact I gained a reputation for this. It was all a considerable responsibility and we had a lot of good luck, but planning was absolutely essential.

As an "extra" to all of this came the Orienteering. Foolishly, I had the impression that it was sort of walking with a compass. I went on a course in Staffordshire where all our outdoor exercises and learning sessions took place in driving sleet. Physically, as I was nearing sixty, I found it all very taxing, particularly sliding down muddy cliffs supposedly in full control.

With Chris S., we started teaching Orienteering back at School. With the eight and nine year olds, we devised three loops at School for seventy children, each taking the hour of their game period. Later, and continuing from this introduction, we borrowed farms, woods and estates for more adventurous courses. It was very hard work, but worth it. We only met one angry farmer and he agreed to join us for tea, so soon forgot the anger.

Both the orienteering and our walks fitted in well with the times. During the last thirty years we all have become more aware of our environment, and we know that we can't take it for granted. The more children, parents and friends who received a taste of walking in and near Oxford, and further afield, the better. They were also important to an understanding of what the School stands for. The children, matrons, stooges, staff, parents and friends all took part in activities together. This meant that we all knew each other, and looked on each other as equals.

Provided we treated the footpath and wilderness areas with respect, and we certainly tried, and we were not prepared to be pushed around by others for their own selfish ends (the farmer and the bridge), we did our bit for goodwill in the community. I used to get parents contacting me and asking me to arrange a walk in their area.

We had also entered into an era where school, parents and children are encouraged to take part in as many positive activities as possible. Quite apart from all this, for those participating, they learn to appreciate the countryside and also to find their way around; in our case in and around Oxfordshire and adjacent counties.

6.   The walk at Great Tew, mid 1980s

7.   Chris, Sue and students lunch on a Sunday walk,
       mid 1980s

8.	Spring in the Chilterns, late 1980s

9.	A wet Spring in Warwickshire, late 1980s

10. Orienteering at Stonesfield, early 1990s

11. Orienteering with Sam, early 1990s

CHAPTER 7

Debating, Drama, Religion and Prizes

Debating

Another area of interest for me was debating, and later, public speaking. For eighty years, before I took on debating, there had been only four masters in charge of this activity (Skipper, Giles, Cecil and Rabbits). This meant that debates were an established part of school life, and the Headmasters and children expected debates to happen.

When I started running the debates, I had not taught English. Later I did, but this really wasn't important. Cecil, who ran the debates for more than twenty years, was a French teacher. In so many schools, debating and public speaking are tied to the English department and run by it. The English department was an important ally as the teachers gave class time for this form of oral English, and that is obviously very important. I always had at least one other colleague to help me to organise debates (Roly, Dougie, Adrian, Bill, Francis, Graham, Adrian or Michael), and we operated outside class time. We conducted about ten debates a year for about ninety minutes, mostly on gloomy Saturday evenings from October to March.

There were two or three speakers on either side of each motion. The most difficult part was actually choosing the motions. Some were irreverent. *"Trash is Bunk"*; *"Homework Should Be Abolished"*; and *"This School Increasingly Resembles A*

Concentration Camp" are three which come to mind!

Others were more serious: *"This House has lost confidence in Her Majesty's Government"*; *"The Police should be armed"*; and *"The best way to preserve the peace is to prepare for war"*. Without doubt the best motion we debated was, *"That this House considers that Euthanasia should be legalised in this country"*. Two of the main speakers have since joined the medical profession so, obviously, they spoke from the heart.

Balloon Debates were great fun. In these, the boys and girls represented various characters, from Sheik Yamani (the Saudi Oil Minister), to Jesus Christ, to Basil Brush (a British children's television puppet) and Florence Nightingale. Harry, one of our best debaters, discovered that he had to be absent on the day of the debate for a family commitment. He took the part of a ghost and together with Desmond, a member of staff, he prepared for the debate. The recording was put through the sound system of the hall. They used a very quiet fan to ruffle a highly visible long curtain at one crucial moment. Harry was many miles away but the audience found his ghostly presence most convincing and voted that he could go into the Balloon! The purpose of the Balloon Debate was to convince the audience that the participants should stay in. The Balloon has set off on a mythical trip to another planet taking with them the best representatives from Earth. It is too heavy and soon starts to sink. Some of the characters must be pushed over the side to be fed to a pack of hungry crocodiles who, in anticipation, have managed to site themselves, jaws snapping, right below the sinking balloon. The debate is about who gets to stay in the Balloon. The audience votes and the results are given the next day at assembly.

We would try to find a time and place to help the principle speakers to prepare. We encouraged speakers to write out their speech in full and then put it on file cards. Scruffy sheets of paper became harder and harder to read, and many memorised their speeches and learned to adapt if they got lost or were interrupted. The standard was remarkably high. What makes a good debate are comments from the floor after the main speeches. We finished with someone summing up for the opposition and then for the motion. I had two clerks to assist who then counted hands for and against, and a result was announced. We had a secretary, who read the minutes of the previous debate, and noted down the present one. To start most debates, the Sergeant-At-Arms (a colleague) asked the audience to stand and the Speaker entered, preceded by the Secretary and Clerks. We, the officials, were dressed in suits, although none of the debaters were. This was all in line with the procedure at the Westminster Parliament.

At all debates, the younger children had their chance. Special debates, excluding those in their last two years, were organised just for them, usually in class time. Of course many of them also attended the School debates as well.

Alexander was one such debater. He was close to being illiterate, had failed the entry exam for his next school, and stayed on an extra term. Any written notes he ever had were merely for show. He couldn't read them either, but with astute waving and reference to them, the act was most convincing. He was articulate and fast off the mark, especially with well-timed interruptions. He deliberately repeated himself, lowered his voice, then raised it again to make a point, and used the debater's pause to great advantage.

I persuaded the Headmaster to award him the major School debating prize at Christmas when he left. Normally it went to a high achiever at the main prize-giving in the summer. He thanked me for the "extra" prize for debating - an impressive and expensive book about horses. Alexander never understood that he had reached the pinnacle. He did not believe he could do well academically. However it was a great strength of the School that it very often found a way for nearly every child to excel in one way or another. Everyone could succeed in something.

Tom, at least ten years after he finished our School, stepped out of a taxi on a crowded road one day and shook me by the hand. Tom, a high achiever, but not one naturally attracted to debating, had been unexpectedly pressed into service when he was still a boy with us. One time I had spotted that there was no one for a scheduled debate in a few days. Roly and I fanned out at the end of the supervised prep and more or less press-ganged some children to become our main speakers. Tom had been swept up in the net, couldn't say no fast enough, and became a regular. When I met him on the road, he had finished school and university and was under contract (at no doubt a considerable salary) to improve the image of a well known oil company. He did this by speaking and making presentations on their behalf throughout the world. It was a considerable compliment to our debating.

The Headmaster and colleagues were always most supportive of debating in every way. The secret was to keep everyone fully informed as far in advance as possible. The children reached a very high standard, and they did so because the School provided them with the opportunity to stand on their own feet, and to speak their own minds. Give them a chance and a challenge and they will take it.

Out of all this came the Public Speaking. For many years at the end of the term, boys and girls were invited to give speeches to an audience at a minor assembly when "Leavers Books" were handed out. Some were good, but most showed a lack of proper preparation, as there appeared to be no guidelines. Some contained very unfortunate language and negative views about members of staff. I cringed with embarrassment. However this was the School's way. The Headmaster preferred this to some regimented and insincere contest. I didn't agree but I kept quiet. There came a time when there were no Leavers speeches because no one wanted to speak.

We then started some proper public speaking. Colleagues were alerted at the start of the School year and asked for their cooperation. The contest would take place towards the end of the second term. Any boy or girl in their final two years could apply. An area of topic - *Great Men, Great Literature, War And Peace, the Advance Of Technology* - was agreed upon. English teachers explained it all to their classes and encouraged entrants.

A month before the finals I took in applications, trying to limit them to twenty. We couldn't handle more. I sent the best ten (or those who were likely to reach the finals) to a panel of professionals to be heard, coached, and finally the best four or five were selected. This panel consisted of friends and colleagues with some experience of speech training. Often one or two helpers from outside the School were included. I dealt with the remainder. Each candidate was heard at least twice and sent away with suggestions for improvement on stance, introduction, voice, content, delivery and conclusion. If, unexpectedly, someone from my group proved better than I had guessed, then of course I sent that child along to be heard by the professionals.

All this needed the cooperation of the games coaches and the Music department and Drama, as there was always a major play at this time.

It all worked surprisingly well. The finalists were chosen a week before the end of term. There was then an opportunity for all to practice, with help, in the School hall. In time they memorised the speeches (I encouraged notes just in case!). All were able to rehearse alone and received guidelines regarding time.

On the day, the whole school gathered for morning assembly as usual. After a hymn, prayer and announcements, the outside judge was introduced. An order of speaking was selected by drawing numbers and we began. It was a large hall and they spoke with no microphone. No shouting, but you must be heard, and right at the back too. We had practiced all this.

I sat near the back holding up a piece of yellow cardboard as a warning that time was nearly up, and, if necessary, showed the other side of the board, which was red (meaning to sit down immediately). The judge retired to consider notes taken, and to decide upon a winner. While this went on, we listened to a student give a piano solo or two students playing violin. Then the judge gave the verdict. The best speech in my time given by Alasdair, and was about the author, Salman Rushdie. He didn't in fact win as he was more than a minute over the agreed time. Perhaps we were over-organised.

Drama

Drama was another activity with which I came to be involved. When I started to take a form (to be a class teacher), we put on minor plays from time to time. We tried to choose plays suitable to the age group as it was essential to have one's class for a large part of their teaching to make this all possible (at least one period per day and preferably some double periods of seventy minutes). The plays needed to be presented, read through, cast and rehearsed.

"Orion and the Dolphin", *"Around the World in Eighty Days"*; *"Bannockburn"* and *"The Secret Life of Walter Mitty"*, come to mind. The children loved to dress up and to perform, especially if there was something exciting on stage like a battle. Passepartout and the Construction of the Gymnastic Pyramid in Japan (a famous episode in Jules Verne's *"Around the World in Eighty Days"*) to suitably taped music, also comes to mind. The appearance of Philaeus Fogg led to the pyramid's collapse and shouts of "Master, Master" from Passepartout. They loved dressing as Indians wearing colourful headdress and brandishing tomahawks ambushed our small party as they crossed the Rocky Mountains by train!

Plays were also a useful distraction. They were good to have up your sleeve if progress in other areas became sluggish. Suddenly the students would become quite articulate and want to learn dialogue by heart.

The Dragon always has a much deserved reputation for producing plays of a very high standard. School plays sometimes were even compared to current professional productions by reviewers.

For forty years, a Shakespeare and a Gilbert and Sullivan play were the two major productions each school year. I never had any doubt that the older children very much appreciated and understood the productions. I was awed by the standards achieved. They were better than anything I had ever seen in a secondary school, much less a prep school.

In time other plays were performed. *"Oliver"*, *"The Beggars Opera"* and *"Charlie's Aunt"* as well as *"Master Beware"*, a play written at the School.

I had never really considered doing a play until one year it looked as if there would be no play if I didn't do it. The "new" School hall built forty five years earlier was being replaced. A new Lynam Hall took its place. There was a gap. A year off? I decided to do the musical, *"The Wizard of Oz"*, in what was known as the old hall. No major play had been performed there for forty six years. It was the original School hall. The acoustics were excellent; it had a high ceiling and stairs descended from the front of the hall, newly built, as a route to some recently constructed classrooms.

There was no stage, only a small platform for the Headmaster to stand on at school assembly. J.R., the resident carpenter, built a sixteen by twenty foot stage and another beside it only a few feet wide. On this at the rear was a small revolving platform: this was divided in four to represent Kansas, Munchkinland, The Dark Forest and The Land of Oz. Granville of the Art staff had produced a miracle. There could be no curtain, so scene changes were made by lowering the lighting. Along with this we accommodated a small orchestra (this area could be entered via a classroom, if a ladder was first climbed to get through the window!).

Mattresses for small children to sit on were placed at the front, and behind them there was room for two hundred spectators. The lights were controlled from a gallery facing the stage. The all-important sound production came from a classroom, windows blackened, and the door opened.

Fortunately Adrian, a new member of staff, who had done much acting in his past, came forward as the artistic director. I cast the main parts with David B. over one lunch break. He casually said that he only had an hour as he was off to London for the rest of the day. Somehow it was all done in that time, and we never had to change a single part or actor. David A. took on the chorus work. Children were placed into two choruses depending on their games group. Half played games on Mondays and Thursdays so they could rehearse on Tuesdays and Fridays. The other chorus did the reverse.

Together with Adrian's help, we edited out a great deal of the play, but added two awesomely awful beasts known as Kalidahs, whom Dorothy and her band met in the forest. Soon I was visited by a delegation of actors and actresses asking us to reinstate all the songs we had cut. So much for keeping the play to a reasonable length! Our sound man, David R., worked with the Wicked Witch of the West who daily became more unpleasant.

Never had I worked so closely and intimately with the children as I did in this play. They were incredible, always cheerful and full of suggestions. The very small aisle acted as the Yellow Brick Road and gave the Scarecrow just enough space to fall over into the Headmaster's lap during a performance, depositing a large amount of straw all over him and his guests.

Towards the end of rehearsals, Dorothy and her little band sped out of the back of the hall on the Yellow Brick Road, across the playground, up some stairs, along a hallway, and re-entered via the stairs above the stage. To get to this entrance, they ran down a corridor by some classrooms where prep was in progress, with Pulley in charge. He, not knowing what was going on, entered just after them. I asked him if he had learned his part: we laughed and he retreated very fast. It was one of the best moments!

As the hall was so open all the time, acting as a passageway and containing six classrooms, later rehearsals were disrupted. But it did introduce the children to the play, and soon a group of small boys pretending they were Munchkins were going through their paces in the playground.

The Major devised a drill for the Oz Army, with one private and three officers. Cindy did masterful choreography with some spooky spectres in the forest, and June worked with the choruses all bunched up on the minuscule stage. Somehow it all happened as planned. All the leading female parts were played by boys so I gave the part of Ozmas, the Oz official, and front man for the Wizard, to Pippa. The Wizard, a very small boy but with a loud voice, was very convincing.

The high drama was produced by the press. Patrick's father was about to be sacked as the head of a TV company's breakfast television show. The press arrived at the play fairly sure Patrick's father would be in the audience. We had him in the green room where the children dress and are made up. David D., another parent (father of Henry, the Lion) and a nationally known TV presenter, promised to deal with them. He did this and Patrick's father slunk into a corner after the play started, sneaking back into the green room for the interval. Despite the length of the play, the Headmaster insisted on a decent interval so that he and his guests could retire to a suitable room nearby for drinks. The play was a great success.

The other major play I produced was *"Bugsy Malone"*. Again I was lucky. The very experienced Michael C., who had recently joined the staff, was installed as artistic director. This was a play I was asked to do. It was a tougher challenge, as I didn't know the play before we started. It was performed in the Lynam Hall with a huge cast. First there were huge financial problems, then there was no musical score. As we felt we had to have an orchestra, David A. organised the writing of the score for which he was quite rightly paid.

I chose a child for a minor part whose father owned a local theatre. He found within his organisation all the hoodlum 1930s outfits. In the final week of rehearsals in the hall, he ask me if there was anything else he could do for us.

"Get us some proper lighting", I said facetiously.

"Right, I will have my man up in the morning", he replied. He was as good as his word. A crew came and lent us some very professional lighting. This was a great improvement as the stage was large and contained Fat Sam's office on an upper level which we could see into only when certain lights were on. All this worked well until just before the final performance when our lighting control panel with its old fashioned rheostats could no longer cope. Mick, our very capable maintenance chief, short-circuited the control panel so all the lights were "on" or "off". We got away with it. The whole evening the stage shone. As most of the audience were parents of the actors, and they love anything their children do, no one said anything. It is very lucky that no electrical inspector was anywhere near!

Then there was the problem of the splurge guns. These gangster tommy guns had to shoot out a stream of foam with the consistency of shaving soap as Fat Sam and his gang eliminated various foes. We found a prototype at an acting club and David R. built six of them. The stage managers had their work cut out to prevent the actors accidentally pressing the trigger backstage during performances.

Fat Sam's rival was Dandy Dan. He suffered a badly broken leg during a ski holiday two months prior to the show. He arrived back at school convinced that he would lose his part. No way. Armed with a cane, a full length walking cast and a wheelchair pushed by flunkeys, he used his disability to great advantage.

I was complimented when casting for including a boy who was ill in sick bay at the time of auditions. As Hugh was in a ground floor sick room he, together with friends, had built a dummy in the bed. He put on his clothes, climbed out the window, attended the audition, was selected, and returned unnoticed to bed. Well done Hugh!

Octavius, whom I badly wanted to audition for a major part, had slipped detention a number of times. By means of some delicate negotiations, I sprung him out of detention for twenty minutes, just long enough to impress the artistic director and nail down the part of Blousey before returning him to finish his extra work. If I remember correctly, I had to supervise the final twenty minutes of detention. The requirements of being the play director were many!

Two weeks before the show there was a hoodlum dance routine which wasn't going well. David B. had to play the piano for this and Cindy, the choreographer had to be there. They had to be on stage to get this routine right. For three weeks they rehearsed this twice a week for twenty minutes. Cindy had to take the part of one of the hoodlum dancers if the dancers were late.

One morning during practice I had forgotten about school assembly and the whole school started to file in, in silence. It was an unexpected public relations coup. At exactly 8.40am the stage curtain pulled shut hiding the dancers, the Headmaster came on stage, and David B. played the morning hymn. After that, the School couldn't wait for the play and neither could we.

After the practices, Fat Sam lost his voice. With his parents safely out of the country (they were there on opening night), we gave him small sips of Port during the play. It did wonders for his voice!

I felt very grateful for the chance to take part in major drama because I was in no way a "professional". Over the years we had several very talented play producers and I admired them all. This gave an entirely different dimension to working with children. The understanding of the play and what it was trying to achieve, had to be total. By that I mean everyone had to work together and there had to be feedback from the children. Sometimes the performance was not quite what the producer intended. I split the jobs of producer and artistic director, simply because with a modern production and many children involved, it became impossible to do both jobs.

Rabbits was excellent with his productions. I admired very much how he produced Macbeth out of doors for the School centenary. The children were so good and so talented that those (and that was most) who acted adult parts put them across convincingly. They couldn't have done this if they hadn't thoroughly understood the play.

For myself I enjoyed working with children in such a unique way. I was very aware that I didn't have an acting background, and at this level it was essential. That is why Adrian and Michael were directors and the Major and Cindy took on special assignments. It was also a chance to work closely with the Music department and this did me a lot of good. I had no musical background at all and I very much came to appreciate the work which they did.

Finally, the children never forgot the experience of acting, working as stage hands and all the essential ingredients which made a good play really successful.

As a postscript, there is also the bizarre and the unexpected. An operetta which I was very interested in as I had twice played a sailor, was *H.M.S. Pinafore.* There is a splendid song sung about Ralph Rackstraw, a British Tar and "Hero" of the play.

> *"For he is an Englishman*
> *and he himself has said it*
> *and its greatly to his credit*
> *that he is an Englishman."*

The part was played by Amedée who had a lovely singing voice. He was French and had come to join us for a couple of terms. He had to be carefully coached on the proper accent for a British Tar, for his natural accent when talking English was very French. The producer stuck to the script. No tricolour and no chorus of La Marseillaise!

Religion

Religion played an important part in school life. We were a Christian school, but we were non-denominational, and we always had a place for other beliefs. There was always a Chaplain who played a full part in the life of the School. The Chaplain took games. Ronnie took Rugby; he was Welsh and he could be very partisan! He came to visit the boarding house in the evening, an event much looked forward to by me, as the children were quiet and there were rugby players in each dormitory. In their lessons, the chaplains taught the children about other religions and explained why we have problems today between religions.

All this was a very big job for the Chaplain and could involve seeing as many as twenty different classes in a week. When it came to exams and report time, this could be a nightmare. Unscrupulous colleagues would insert bogus written exams or report forms for non-existent children.

Provision was made for the Catholics. They went to Mass in town most Sundays at the same time the rest of us were at the School service. In addition, we always provided a quiet room for those being prepared for their Bar Mitzvah.

Robert Runcie, a parent, who went on to become the Archbishop of Canterbury, gave the best explanation of our Sunday Service when he spoke at the School Centenary Service.

"For a hundred years, you have resisted building a Chapel; for nearly a hundred years your changeless Sunday Services have been unique. Those invited to speak at them must remember a sentence in the Hobbit "It is not difficult to make a slip when

talking to Dragons!" Yet the object of this tradition has been to keep religion at the heart of your life, and not to lock it up in a separate slot."

Each Sunday, a wooden cross was lowered to the centre of the stage in the School hall. Rosemary, the Domestic Bursar, provided a variety of splendid flower arrangements to each side.

The boarders all attended, as well as many parents and day boys and girls. The choir (senior and junior) treated us to anthems from time to time. The senior choir included a dozen or so adults as well as the boys and girls.

The heart of the service was the children's readings. They put much thought and effort into these and all read beautifully and convincingly. The Chaplain preached once a term, as did one of the Headmasters. Members of staff also preached. There was a wide variety of visitors who came to speak too. Once a year, we went to a local church for the carol service and to Christ Church Cathedral, Oxford, where we joined in a service with the congregation from the College.

During my travels, I was asked to preach four times. My themes were: *Fishing, Thanksgiving, Jackie Robinson the baseball star* and *Every school has a soul.*

To rescarch Jackie Robinson, I visited the archives of the Montreal Gazette and was photographed with a snow covered statue of him, now situated at the entrance to the Olympic Stadium. I was twelve when Jackie, in order to break the colour bar, played a season for the Montreal Royals.

It was essential to speak for no more than twelve minutes and preferably to learn it all by heart. It was a difficult task. I wasn't used to it, but the Chaplains were always very supportive.

At the end of The Great War (W.W.I), when many old boys had been killed in action, there was a move to build a Memorial Chapel. The Headmaster, the Skipper, decided instead on a Memorial Cross by the river. On the Sunday nearest to 11 November, Remembrance Sunday, we went every year for a memorial service. This was very moving. It started with a minute's silence, following the firing of a cannon a mile away in the City Centre.

As a newly-arrived member of staff, I had had to help to drag a piano across the playing fields to this muddy location. In later years, Scotty and his Brass Group would provide the music for the hymns and also the *"Last Post"*. Sometimes a wreath was laid, usually by a relative of someone killed in one of the Wars. Hundreds attended, all wearing their poppies, the symbol of the Great War from the carnage in Flanders Fields. There were readings and hymns, and on one occasion, an old boy, a well known poet, recited a poem he had written some years after he had been a boy at a service in Skipper's time. It was about this service and he called it "No Ordinary Sunday". That it was not. For years I was asked what church service I attended while at Oxford, and I simply said the school service. I had to explain that it had its own form and meaning, and I always asked the questioner to come with me if they were ever in Oxford on a Sunday and then they would understand. It was the School community coming together to worship in its own way. Loosely Anglican, but really non-denominational.

Prizes

Most years I attended the School prize giving. The various prizes for all the activities within the School were given on the last full school day in July. Usually this was on a Monday. Prizes for the Athletics which finished two days earlier could then be included.

I once asked a parent if she didn't find it inconvenient having it on a Monday. After all both she and her husband had to work very hard to afford the School fees. "Don't ever change from doing it this way", was the reply. In their diaries, both she and her husband had blocked off this day, and the following one as well, when they collected their sons and took them home. It was part of school and family life.

The prize giving was very much for the children. The School resisted the temptation to make it an occasion to impress the parents with long lists of accomplishments of the year. No visiting headmaster to sound off about trends in education, instead a mother and a father of two leavers came to give away the prizes and to speak to us. Their remarks were very much directed at the children. Some were distinguished people and others just good, loving, parents who had never previously spoken in public. Here are some gems from what they said:

"At this school there is a complete contempt for authority coupled with an abiding helpfulness to strangers."

" The children here are no respecters of persons, but they do respect people"

" The relationship existing between students and staff is to be envied by any schoolmaster in the world."

"Games help develop closeness between student and teacher. Seeing a teacher on the playing field running around with his students makes him (or her) a far more real person than just seeing them in the classroom."

"Some people don't agree with prize giving. One is applauding excellence."

"Bad schools make children into little identikits. You are encouraged to be himself or herself."

A mother remembers watching rugby when her son first arrived at school:

"I saw a motley band of some of the muddiest, scruffiest, untidiest small boys - it was a quality of radiant happiness which shone through the murkiness of that grey afternoon."

She then went on to say, *"The band of scruffs are allowed to address their teachers in a way which must baffle poor old foreigners."*

The Headmasters did pass on the occasional gem also, but kindly directed most of what they had to say to staff who were leaving.

<u>From Inky:</u>   *"The School is becoming too conventional. We shall have to do something about it."*

<u>From Joc:</u> (a) *"Happiness is based on freedom. You can't let people down without endangering happiness or freedom."*

     (b) *"The thing about children here that amazes me is the way they always have such nice manners considering how rude the Headmaster can be."*

     (c) *"You must challenge customs and conventions. I had almost said traditions which have already* outlived their usefulness."

The staff didn't escape either. Once, after several busy days and late nights, I was spotted by a father who concluded his remarks by saying; *"Well there is poor old Bev nodding off. Obviously it is time that I sat down."*

On another occasion when the academic cups, books, athletic shields and other prizes had been given out, a father said, *"Oh, I am sorry Bev. You look pretty bored. I have a little prize for you."* I had to walk some distance to reach the platform and to be presented with a Mars bar.

My travels took me to some pretty strange places!

12. Early days in the Lynam Hall, early 1990s

13. Relaxing after the end of term, 1980s

CHAPTER 8

Beyond the Classroom

One event, occurring only twice a year, had a profound influence on the whole school. This was the Sing Song. This doesn't sound earthshaking but it was. Nothing prepared me quite for this. I had attended Sing Song at camp as a child, where we all gathered around the campfire trying to stay warm and to sing contemporary songs.

This event took place in the old hall. To make it difficult, there was no stage, only a stand and platform. It was only possible to get to the platform once the Sing Song had started by climbing a ladder, through a high window and "on stage" through a classroom at one side. The ladder was in semi-darkness and there was a jump to the floor from the window sill.

The boys and a few girls started off with a selection of well known songs; often with words referring to contemporary events at school. *"Old MacDonald"*, *"The Drunken Sailor"*, *"Oh Dooda Day"*, *"This Old Man"* are songs that come to mind. *"Inky Pinkey Parlez Vous"* was another. The compere worked the audience into a good mood. After half an hour of singing, then the Sing Song went up a gear to the staff acts.

It is rather dated now, but the following act created a very strong impression on me at the time. Remember that the Classics dominated the timetable, so the children fully understood exactly what Jacko, the compere, meant as he spoke in Latin (I didn't, as I knew no Latin).

He was a very senior Master having then served nearly forty years on the staff. He came on stage in a suit, gown and mortarboard. From a clipboard, he read the first Latin sentences.

Latin: "Romani in Galliam processerunt."

English: "The Romans advanced into Gaul."

Some scruffy Gauls dressed in old sheets fled before a Roman chariot drawn by soldiers. Other Romans in splendid uniform (no doubt borrowed from the School wardrobe collection) flailed the Gauls with swords.

Latin: "Romani terram vastaverunt."

English: "The Romans laid waste the countryside."

The soldiers chased sheet-clad Gaul women (played by Matrons) around the hall shouting bloodthirsty threats.

Latin: "Gallise collegerunt et Romanos e patria expulerunt."

English: "The Gauls rallied and swept the Romans out of their country."

Now the Gauls all reappeared armed with soda siphons. The Romans retreated in great disorder, upsetting the chariot.

Jacko looked as if he was about to read the next sentence when one Gaul appeared from a nearby classroom and squirted him neatly in the face, suit, gown, mortarboard and all. This was the end of the act. It impressed me because no matter how senior and awe-inspiring some of the senior staff were to me, and no doubt to many children as well during the School term, they also positively relished the chance for a bit of slapstick at the Sing Song. It showed that there was no place for pomposity or hubris. This is an essential thing to remember if a teacher is to be a success.

Later Jacko appeared dressed as a French Canadian Coureur de Bois, with a plaid cloth jacket and fur hat, and with his ukulele, played *"Olga Polouski"*, and *"Jean Baptiste and his Doggie"*.

Joc as Headmaster came on to round out the evening. He sang a song about *"The School along the Bardwell Road"* to his own words and very much reflecting what had happened that term. We then linked hands and sang *"Auld Lang Syne"* which means long ago, and went off to unwind before bed.

In later years, Inky, at every summer term end Sing Song, appeared with Guv, dressed as Lady Bougainvillea. This character represented the fictitious large-bosomed mother, dressed in a large floral "Frock", as the visiting mother at prize giving. Some prizes were then presented, Inky reading the citation and Guv making the presentation, usually with large kisses on both cheeks for the unfortunate prize winner.

The prize might be the old case from a stop watch to aid punctuality, given to a member of staff (or boy) who was far too often late, or a face cloth to a boy (or girl) whose cleanliness was in question. I was given an awful pair of worn out gym shoes for "running walks".

There were serious music items. Ian, who ran an optional activity called "Jive", was brilliant and showed off his talent for singing and dancing with a supporting caste of matrons and secretaries. Tony, who was a great character, came on wearing an old raincoat and carrying a helium-filled balloon as he whistled *"The Blue Danube"*.

The Chaplain, Ronnie, sang a song about the ladies, *"Ma Escritt She's The One For Me But Lets Not Forget Ma Vickers Too"*.

Once a year I did a routine with Roly, *"Squishy squishy squishy ya ya boo ya boo squishy and a squish to you"* we then squished a few and finished with:

Hip hip hooray the holidays are here
The boys can have the lollipops
The staff can have the beer

(Sometimes the other way around)

Once I was on a plane to Kenya during the Sing Song. Roly and I prepared the usual sort of routine and put it all on tape. Roly then constructed a fantastically complicated radio receiver on stage and led the audience through the act. So adept was he that most if not all actually thought I was coming in from far over the Mediterranean!

"Yes, Roly, I can hear you, I am just having another daiquiri." Those in authority (I was told upon my return) became irritated as the time we took was far beyond what was normally allowed. Roly, oblivious to hints that it might be time to wrap up, kept going until the beer and lollipops.

The legacy of the Sing Song was the fact that the children and staff laughed together. It was not a case of the children laughing at the staff. It is important to make this distinction. Of course the incidents quoted above are of another era, but self-parody is one of the greatest forms of humour. There was no place for pomposity but at the same time, no respect was lost. I believe that the Sing Song was more important than any of us realised at the time.

At Christmas there was a different sort of Sing Song. During the final week of term there were two carol services. One was a formal affair held in a local church. The other was the community carols held in the very large Lynam Hall. For this we were all jammed in with the school choir of children and adults, and an orchestra of children in our midst.

We sang some carols together, but there some exceptions. On the twelfth day of Christmas my true love gave to me, and on through the fifth day brought amazing leaping and singing. We were told if we were to be a French Hen or a Leaping Lord, and we had to act and sing the part. An element of laughter crept in, and the crowd gradually warmed up. By the end of this concert the music director had one section of the room singing one line, and the section opposite the next. All of us sang, and hopefully we didn't shout. Any formality at the beginning of the evening soon melted away.

The single activity which did so much to reinforce the positive atmosphere was the dancing. As the School Dance happened during the same week at the end of the Christmas Term as the Charity Sale, I wasn't involved with the dance. Once I was kitted up as Santa Claus to distribute gifts. I don't know if it was because I had the wrong kind of Ho! Ho! Ho! or not, but I was never asked again.

When I arrived, dancing had been a part of school life for several decades. Two nights a week, from September to December, instruction was given to the whole school and was compulsory for boarders. Many day boys, their sisters and the girls from a school nearby were included. The lessons took place during prep. Children danced, then did prep, or the other way around. Some even danced between two sessions of prep. June, Sarah and their faithful crew of dance teachers, with Harry on the piano, had to be good or the whole thing would have been a shambles. Aided by Putty and the prep supervisors, crowd control was maintained. They learned ballroom dances including the Waltz as well as the Foxtrot, Polka and even the Charleston. Harry took a more advanced group for Scottish Dancing where they learned how to dance the Gay Gordons and other reels.

On the last night of the Christmas Term the dance took place. An orchestra of music teachers, staff, and friends practiced the night before. The School hall was decorated including a Christmas tree, streamers and coloured lights.

The youngest children had the first hour, including a visit with Santa. They then went to a smaller hall for the conjurer's show and a film. Nearby there was a buffet to follow. The older children, some in fancy dress, took over the dance floor. Many staff and matrons joined in. There were special elimination dances, intervals for the orchestra to rest, and towards the end the reels. Judges were present to choose the best dancers, prizes to be awarded at the time, and a grand prize at the school prize giving. The only groans came when it all came to an end.

Thus the first term, a long and tiring one, ended on a happy note. As with the Sing Song, the dancing and the School Dance were a coming together. We were all equals again and it did much to reinforce a feeling for the School and to increase everyone's respect for it as an institution.

Every year at the end of the summer term, came the boys and girls' River Regatta. This was a Regatta for the leavers and there were punt races, canoeing contests and the star attraction, the "Greasy Pole".

A thick pole covered in grease was suspended over the River Cherwell. A boy or girl would then advance from each end and would try to wrestle the other so that one fell off into the river while the other remained on the pole. The winner of the round then faced another opponent and so on. Usually after a couple of victorious rounds, the victor would fall off too, so everyone had a chance.

I well remember one leaver, who had been summoned that day to meet the Housemaster of his next school, was desperate to get back in time. This took careful planning. I placed large orange cones on the Bardwell Road to make sure his mother could instantly park her car. She drove at breakneck speed and on arrival, her son had finished the change from his best suit into swimming gear. He raced for the river just in time! These term end events meant a great deal to these leavers.

Every other year following the boys Regatta there was the Grand Rag Regatta which was an extra item performed by the staff. Some of these were quite spectacular and well rehearsed. There was a theme, *"Columbus and 1992"*, *"It's a knockout"* and *"Omelette"* (in the place of Hamlet) are some that come to mind.

A staff organiser, usually the author, acted as compere, explaining all with the help of a hand-held megaphone. With the river so handy, actors were conveniently disposed of into the water.

My favourite, which alas I was only able to watch, was the battle between the Vikings and Saxons. The former, in a punt in dress uniform complete with twin horned helmets and battle axes, were attacked by Saxons in row boats wearing sackcloth. The latter let fly with bags of flour which split, so filling the surroundings with a thick white fog. The Vikings were supposed to win and in the end only one white coated warrior remained in the punt.

During *"Omelette"* Horatio was challenged to a duel. Edward, a member of staff and a former Olympic fencer, challenged Horatio. There was a bank of twenty five feet from the playing field to the river bank. They rolled and clashed swords. In the end the challenger was seen off.

There were river edge disasters. Ladders fell over with characters clinging to them, and even an old bicycle ridden down the bank and along an old diving board and into the river at speed.

Guv dressed as Queen Boadicea, in an outfit similar to that he wore in the evening as Lady Bougainvillea, was deposed and pushed into the river.

This no doubt just seems funny and foolish. It was however a great deal more and it never could have taken place if we didn't have a great confidence in the School. And it showed us at our best, never too grand to face humiliation and never too filled with self importance. The children who were to leave us for good the next day went away with unforgettable memories.

The School had unique staff outings. Joc had sometimes taken some of us to the races or to Henley for the Regatta. This was his way of saying "Thank You" for going that extra mile.

Inky preferred the annual Rugby match between Oxford and Cambridge which took place in early December at Twickenham. The Rugby ground was surrounded by car parks in fields where there might be grass, but in a wet year, also mud. A Land Rover or school minibus set out during the morning with the caterer, a driver and the Headmaster. They then set up tables, chairs and even an umbrella. The "hot box" contained a hot lunch of rice and chilli con carne. Drinks, snacks and plates were laid out. A feast in December? The staff arrived as soon as they could get away from school.

Friends, former parents, Heads and staff of other schools all came to have a drink or some hot soup with us. Stories were swapped and a very good time had over two hours. It was in fact a public relations coup. How much easier in future to approach someone first met at Twickenham as Charlie and not Mr. Jones. This sort of connection did the School a lot of good.

We packed up the lunch in time, all attended the match and found our way back to the School for evening duty. There was always a Corporal's Guard back on the Bardwell Road with a full program of events for the afternoon. For those not watching the match on television, there were vol games (vol meaning voluntary) and Pirates in the School gym with Pulley. Many children attended matches with their parents and friends. Any day children whose parents both worked stayed at school until the normal departure time.

We never had to pay anything on that day. The Headmaster, Bursar and School gave us a day out to remember.

Although I was involved in a wide range of activities at the school, the only one which I fundamentally altered was the Annual Christmas Charity Sale.

Going back to the 1940s, collections were taken at the School plays and the proceeds given to charity. As time went on, it was clear that the School should be doing more.

The School is a Charitable Trust. It has a Board of Governors and is non-profit making. Therefore it is exempt from most taxes levied on property and business and does not have to pay any value added taxes. To continue to justify this status, it was very helpful to be seen to be doing positive work on behalf of deserving charities.

Here we did get the children involved. It was important that they were aware that charitable giving is not just donating money. To have a good sale requires much effort by many. The activities offered where they could also participate were effective and fun. No one from among the children was forced to take part.

The money made as profit was never large in the initial years, usually less than £500 annually, it was only when the size and scope increased that profits increased to £2,000 a year by the middle of the 1970s. By the late 1990s, the profits approached £40,000 annually.

In the 1950s Joc, together with Joyce, the senior matron, made the sale into something with a shape to it and it was fun. The children were involved in the final run up to the sale and the running of the stalls. Joc, a great showman, was brilliant on the day.

By the 1960s, the sale was largely centred on the old hall and adjacent playground. Joc would come out of one of the classrooms, mount the platform and, waving an old golfing umbrella, urge us all to buy more raffle tickets, or to visit the ladies stall.

Proceedings concluded with the draw of the raffle tickets. The stalls were all run by staff and they were also involved in producing what was sold. Dear Pat B., our Biology teacher, met with a group of ladies once a week throughout the term to sew and make clothes for the ladies stall.

Soon after I became involved, we invited three parents to join the sale committee. This helped to produce goods for sale and in subsequent years the numbers of parents involved went up, making the preparations better organised and as we had early meetings in May or June, we developed a "sense of purpose".

For six years, during the Christmas term, I had a small sale optional activity of a dozen children. We spent weeks (and not just at the normal activity time) preparing items. We picked blackberries for jam and jelly. One year we made a very good harvest from a crab-apple tree. We cooked them and put the pulp in a muslin bag. The juice which slowly dripped through was made into jelly. The mess in the School kitchen over several days meant we were not encouraged to repeat this.

Each year we collected pots, bulbs and fibre and planted up to one hundred pots of hyacinths, tulips and daffodils. They were stored on the floor of Roly's garden shed in the dark to grow roots. Brought into the light a week before the sale, the pots were decorated with colored paper and moss to protect the new shoots.

A friend gave us sacks of lavender each year. We had work parties to strip the lavender from each branch and to put it into little bags. We also stuffed sausage dog doorstops with clean sand. A parent with a flair for decoration helped us make attractive Christmas tree decorations using twigs, bull rushes, plasticine and red, green, silver and gold spray paint.

During the final weeks of the School year we picked strawberries, gooseberries and red and black currants. The fruit was taken to Annette, a hard working parent, to make jams. We had a massive bottle drive and the School caterer provided sugar.

I aimed at one thousand jars, a total we never reached, but we came close.

There was always a move to have a stall with goods the children could afford and also games that they could play. The Science Club had a marvellous old crane made from Meccano which we lovingly repaired and kept going for years. Simple toys were made using pipe cleaners.

All donations we couldn't find a home for, we sent to the White Elephant stall. There Chris and Tony K., aided by boy volunteers and much loud touting about the bargains available, got rid of old ski poles, typewriters and even some school furniture by arrangement with the Bursar. Guv's winter overshoes, gathered up from under the stairs where he lived, were sold here. He noted this very quickly and I was lucky enough to find the purchaser, buy them back and return them to their normal place. He told me that they were sold again the next year but I didn't believe him.

We created a Tunnel of Horrors. Absolute darkness was essential which we had in our changing room. A tape with Frankenstein and Dracula voices, screams and laughter, interspersed with pistol shots, greeted the visitor. They felt an eye ball which was a peeled grape, walked (or tried to) on banana skins, had to push through weighted shoe laces, walked on glass (actually potato crisps) and met with wet and slimy curtains.

One parent complained to me that her son had entered this tunnel, but never came out. How could I find out what had happened to him? I assured her he was O.K. I assumed he had used the tunnel to give her the slip.

There was face painting and games in the gym with Pulley. We made popcorn and candy floss, hot dogs and mulled wine for the adults. A second-hand book stall produced one or two first editions and an author found that a recently published and signed book he had written, he could buy back for ten pence. Other authors signed copies of their books with a personalised comment for a fee.

The sale was opened by a visitor giving a short talk in the playground as the School bell sounded. It finished with the raffle and an auction; needed as we received so many quality contributions. A London Committee was created. We needed more quality wine for the bottle stall. The trick was to get hold of the secretary where the parents worked and have our name added to their list of business gifts at Christmas. We also promised to collect, and were soon inundated with cases of vintage wine. I wrote to many mothers asking them to bake us a cake. These were very popular and sold early.

It was left to the Headmaster, aided by some parents, to decide which charities we would support. Many were ongoing. Most were local and connected with helping children, particularly those with a disability or suffering as a result of disease. One year he sent us to visit a charity to which we had contributed. I went with the children of the Sale Optional Activity Group to the south coast to see some recently-arrived orphans from the Vietnam War. It was a bleak, clammy winter day and they were lying in an old army camp. We all wished that we had done more for them.

The Headmaster provided Henry, a university undergraduate whose term end preceded ours by ten days, as a sale stooge. He was good for me as he always asked awkward questions where others would never dare. We became firm friends. Both Henry and his successor, David R. (who later joined the staff), were young and able to do the physical moving and carrying which became too much for me.

There came a point when I had to give it up, at least the running of the sale. I wrote a manual on how it should be done which my successors disposed of without causing offence. Having the chance to do this work, so admirably started by Joc, was something I was always grateful to Inky for making possible. The sheer size of it all and all my demands must have put quite a strain on the smooth running of the School. He never complained and interfered hardly at all, and I am sure that he covered up for my inadequacies.

14. The Greasy Pole, late 1970s

15. In Sing Song mode, early 1980s

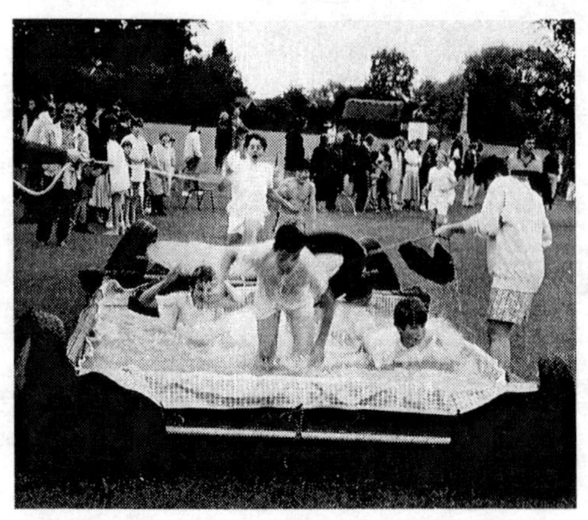

16. The obstacle course at the athletics end of the school
     year, late 1980s

17. The Grand Day Regatta at the end of the Summer term

18. The Grand Day Regatta at the end of the Summer term

19. The planting of bulbs for the Christmas Charity Sale, late 1980s

20. Collecting holly for the Charity Sale, late 1980s

21. Scotty and a Summer Walk, late 1980s

CHAPTER 9

Play

Shortly after Ronnie, our Chaplain, arrived at the School, he was being shown around by Bleachy, a staff member who was acting as his "pater", As they crossed the playground talking to each other, a cricketer who was involved in a game with his friends, sharply hit a tennis ball which ricochetted off his leg.

Ronnie turned to the boy and said, "Can't you see what you are doing? You should be more careful."

As they rounded the next corner, Bleachy said, "Remember it's their playground." Ronnie had learned a valuable lesson which he never forgot.

Play is crucial to children's development. It is important to let them develop as children, to provide the best playgrounds possible, and then to leave them alone to get on with it.

We had a problem. Modern demands of education led to playground restrictions. There was nowhere else to go. New modern classrooms and laboratories had to be built.

One large area, which had been a number of grass tennis courts, was converted into an "all-weather surface." Provided we all wore the correct boots and running shoes and no mud came near, we could go onto its surface. This took some pressure off the playground.

It is crucial that children play. This takes many forms. For physically active play, they get exercise, especially important when there are time consuming academic demands. Play can be quiet, a game of cards or chess in a classroom, or Dungeons and Dragons in a corner of the library. It can also be destructive. There must be some adult supervision which the children respect. Rules should be kept to a minimum, but these must be enforced. Above all play gives children the ability to get on with others. The rapport between teachers on playground duty and the children was good. Any bullying could be noticed and stopped before it started. Also if the children are positively occupied, then there is no place for bullying.

Many times I was on playground duty brought me into close contact with every sort of problem. We tried to ban as little as possible. If matches or bangers (fire crackers) appeared they were seized. Some children pinched drawing pins and hammered them into the soles of their shoes. Then they could slide easily on smooth surfaces. This was stopped as were all manner of pea-shooters and spit balls which could make a mess of the classroom walls.

The classrooms mostly remained open as a base for day boys and girls. The form teacher had to create his or her standards there, and to lay down what activities could and could not take place, as well as whether visitors were allowed in, how many and when. The children never minded the form teacher being there correcting, changing the wall display or writing work on the board.

Once by chance, from my window in the boarding house, I saw through a high window into a classroom in the old hall across the lane. I saw a scene I will never forget. It looked as if there was a game of "Strip Poker" in progress. Music faintly reached me out of the open window opposite. I fetched a couple of colleagues as we considered how to handle this.

In the end it was decided that they would go into the old hall and stand by the door to the classroom which was presumably closed. One shouted to the other to meet him in the playground. The familiar adult voice through the door brought instant results. The miscreants dressed in remarkable time. Nothing further was said obviously, though one of us did say sometime later to the boy we saw with most of his clothes off, that it was always a good thing to keep one's clothes on in the classroom. Otherwise they might get lost! The point had been made and I assume the message was received as there were no further occurrences. We alerted the form teacher!

Marbles dominated the start of the School year with cries of "Roll Up Roll Up" all around the playground. Wherever there was a backstop four tich (small marbles) would be laid as a simple pyramid in a dip. The object was to hit the pyramid and dislodge the marbles. If you did you took the four marbles, if you missed you lost yours. If you hit the pyramid, but it didn't move, then you could try again. The correct technique was to stand with your legs apart and your arms outstretched, swinging a number of times before letting go. This is much as a golfer with practice swings before addressing the ball, or a curler or bowler prior to releasing the throw. There were a variety of marbles, semis, big semis, spirals, medium and jumbo triple treb marbles.

Marbles were then followed by Conkers and a different cry rang out, "Any one take me on Onkers?"

Once the chestnuts started to fall from the trees, as autumn advanced, they were eagerly collected, the prickly outside being cut away. The chestnut had a hole drilled in it and a string with a knot put through the hole. The string was slightly more than a foot and a half in length. The object was to swing your conker on its string at the opponent's held vertical and stationary. If you hit, you tried again and again. A miss and it was the opponent's turn. The object was to break the conker of your opponent so it fell to the ground in bits. The victor, like a fighter pilot in war time, would keep track of the kills, so a "twoer" in time became a "sixer" or higher. "Loser picks up the bits", we would be reminded from time to time at morning assembly.

Bad Eggs and Lurky were two games where a "pitch" or play area had to be quickly "bagged" at the start of a playtime. For Bad Eggs, a tennis ball was thrown against a wall and a name shouted. If it was Smith, he had to catch the ball before it bounced or with "one hand, one bounce." Then he could return the favour to someone else, otherwise the throw reverted to the starter. This game helped to develop great skills at throwing accurately and with pace and also a quick pick-up. Useful for cricket?

In Lurky, a block was placed and two circles drawn, usually with white chalk borrowed from a classroom. A boy designated as "he" protected the block. Others hid. The object was to try to get to the block and kick it before being noticed. If the "he" shouted "Lurky Jones" before Jones kicked the block, then Jones had to go to a second circle where he could be rescued by one of the other players touching him in the circle before being noticed. It is a good game in which it paid the attackers to coordinate their plans.

The pièce de résistance was Warning. Coppers, the most energetic of Masters, was an expert. Everyone hides in an agreed area. This time the "he" (usually Coppers) races and catches one player by touching him. They then hold hands and attack together. Soon there are three, four, six, ten holding hands. The attackers now move more slowly. In wet weather it was played indoors in the old hall with its classrooms off at the sides. The chain would race at speeds - it had to stop if any hands parted - up and downstairs, along passages and in and out of classrooms until there was only one boy not caught. We would all then collapse from exhaustion.

There were more organised games indoors for days with bad weather. Pirates in the gym with all the apparatus out. Those chasing and being chased had to leap, swing and jump without hitting the floor.

In the old hall, Battlefields was played. This was a game played by equal sides, up to twenty a side, with light rubber soccer-sized balls. I learned this during a years exchange in New York. There, any outdoor fields among the sky scrapers were at a premium, so various indoor games, improvised and taking place in rented indoor facilities, were necessary. The old hall was quite small, so it was hard to react in time to a ball thrown at you.

The object was to hit an opponent and put him out of the game. If on the other hand, one caught an opponent's throw, then the thrower was out. The referee had to be alert. Lines in chalk were drawn across the floor to mark "ends" and a neutral zone. Those hit or caught retreated to the sidelines. In the final phase the referee shouted, "Advance into enemy territory." The action was then not limited, so the chasers chased or were chased until one side was eliminated.

One autumn term in the late 1970s, skateboards appeared. Every boy and girl wanted one. The playground was ideal, quite smooth (there were rough patches which became rougher as the term progressed). There were informal races, slalom and jump skill testing sessions, and the more expert travelled by skateboard from one classroom to another carrying books. In the classroom they were a problem as storage space was very limited. Some of my colleagues weren't too careful where they stepped when teaching and paid the price.

If they weren't going to be banned, then there would have to be some controls. I took on the job of registering them. The wheels had to be firmly attached and working. Then the owner was given a stick-on label firmly put in place with layers of sellotape. Non-registered boards were confiscated.

The Doctor, tired from repairing injured knees and elbows, decreed that knee and elbow pads must be worn. He would have preferred helmets as well, but this wasn't practical. The number of skateboards at School fell. The craze passed for a time, without skateboards having to be banned.

About ten years later a new kind of roller skate burst on the scene. With the all-weather area these roller blades became popular. There were some hockey pickup games using ice hockey sticks. We also had a slalom course on a sloping section of the playground and every so often a marathon. Our playground had many small buildings so spectators had to stand well back. Skateboards made a comeback.

During the wet and dank winter term we had a collection of very worn field hockey sticks, so hockey of a sort took place in the playground using tennis balls. The maintenance staff put wire covers over the most vulnerable windows.

When better weather came, old cricket bats made their appearance, with improved stumps. Once I foolishly attempted to carry six good wine glasses across the playground held up on a tray. A wet finger drawn around the rim caused a hum, valuable for a Physics lesson. I was convinced that there was no chance that a tennis ball would hit. I was wrong. The amazing thing is that no glasses broke, they just fell over on the tray.

I met Julian in the playground. I never taught him or had him in any activity so I only saw him at play. He was the most memorable and endearing child of my time. He was a haemophiliac. This meant he bruised and bled easily and spent periods in hospital receiving blood and "resting", so the bleeding would die down. His parents wanted him to have as near-normal a childhood as possible.

He couldn't take part in any of the organised physical activity or sport in the gym or on the fields. He did swim for his form in the swimming relays, but no jumping into the pool. In the playground he was in his element. He was a forceful and positive person, so a good organiser. He was always was at the centre of most "unofficial" games. He would get friends to push his wheelchair at speed, in circles and with rather sudden stops. He would emerge sometimes with a crutch to help him and disappear into a building. We had to keep a close watch on him, but try not to stop his fun. He missed some school, but academically he was quite able and he sang well. He threw himself into everything he did with gusto. His time with us was memorable, as it was for everyone he came across.

Years later when Julian had grown up, he acquired AIDS from an infected blood transfusion. He campaigned on behalf of all sufferers, who had contracted the disease or were H.I.V. positive. This big effort on his part brought some compensation for sufferers, alas after Julian's premature death.

My travels in the playground are the most important part of my journey. Again the Headmaster took the risks and left play to develop and become a central part of what the children learned and retained when they left us.

22. Stilt walking, the Centenary, 1977

23. A marathon on roller skates, late 1980s

CHAPTER 10

Governors, Inspectors and the School

The Governors and Bursar also had their part to play. The cost of all the "free range" activities and occasional damage, however unintentional, must have caused concern. It was certainly a cost worth paying.

A parent on speech day put it so well. "I suppose there is a governing body. I know nothing about it. I have never heard anything about it, but if it exists, I think it must be a jolly good one, because it clearly gives the impression that the place is run by and belongs to the boys and girls, assisted by the Masters, and that seems to me to be exactly as it should be."

This was not quite true for the staff. The Bursar was responsible directly to the Governors, in fact he acted as Secretary to the Board. We felt at times that the Headmasters were being undermined.

Frank was a remarkable Bursar. We did enjoy seeing him "hopping mad" at times, but he had to keep the School on an even keel. He somehow kept the "show on the road". It can't have been easy at times because the Headmasters always seemed to approve any reasonable request. It was probably a good thing he was responsible to the Governors, as it gave him some way of restricting us when we tried to spend too much School money. One bone of contention in many schools is salaries. They were always discussed, including extras for this and that, but we followed the national teachers' scale known as Burnham very closely, and had surprisingly little dissension as a result.

Towards the end of my time at the School, the staff had a governor directly representing their interests. This was a positive step. Personal problems concerned with employment could be considered. Also this governor could canvass staff views on the appointment of a new Headmaster.

Inspections and inspectors, in their own way, played a part. My first encounter with inspectors came unexpectedly and I made some mistakes which were all my fault. Shortly after my arrival, Joc asked me to pour drinks and to welcome a conference of school doctors meeting at the Dragon School. Naturally they asked me questions, and I said I was amazed that the School had "a plunge" in the boarding house. We didn't have anything like that at home. Every boy in the morning had to plunge into this lead-lined bath of cold water. Recently there were too many leaks to repair so it had been shut down. It hadn't been removed. The doctors were intrigued by this story and pulled the leg of the Headmaster about it.

"Kindly stick to what I asked you to do", Joc said as the last doctor departed. I wasn't asked to help entertain dignitaries again.

Next came Lady Plowden. She called at the School and asked to see me. I think she wanted to talk to someone fairly recently arrived. We talked about what I found here in comparison with Canada. I am glad to say that nothing I said went into the Plowden Report on Education which had an impact in Britain at the time. She took with her a game of mine, "Mango" (a sort of Mathematical bingo), which was returned with thanks.

There were other inspections by individuals or groups on behalf of the Ministry or the Prep School Association. They disapproved of our rather run down classrooms (from over use), lack of display space, or good writing boards. They seemed to like everything else. Ann, a Science colleague had a six month old baby as an exhibit for her Biology lesson. The inspectors, completely mesmerised by the baby's winning smile, wrote a glowing report about the entire Science department. Well done Ann!

On another occasion, due to a misunderstanding about dates, the entire final year was absent for the inspection. I didn't teach this group on the day in question, but the Headmaster insisted I accompany them for their expedition. According to colleagues, I was considered too controversial so best off the premises. During this visit, one inspector took a liking to one of the high tall-backed master's chairs in one of the empty classrooms. A boy was delegated to carry this chair from class to class during the day, so the inspector could sit looking over the back of the class!

Major school events contributed to life at the School. Three times I attended the Royal Tournament at Earls Court in London. The entire School, including secretaries, maintenance staff, dailies, matrons and all the children and staff went by double-decker bus from the Bardwell Road to the railway station where we boarded a special Dragon Express. This took us to Kensington Olympia. From there it was a short walk to the show. There was a lot of room to move around, when we were not in our own section. The trip home was great fun. Somehow the railway caterers provided packed lunches and on the return journey, the Headmaster arranged for a refreshment compartment for the staff.

We organised all kinds of daily expeditions throughout the country. A whole age group would go to London for the day. When we reached Paddington, we were divided so to visit the Tower of

London, the Mint, the Zoo, museums and galleries, all meeting on a staggered timetable for lunch, swapping groups and going off for afternoon trips before finally meeting at Paddington for the return trip. We made a similar trip to Cardiff once, our time spent visiting iron and steel works as well as castles.

Chris organised many visits to HMS Dolphin, the submarine training tower at Gosport, to the Mary Rose and HMS Victory at Portsmouth. I was lucky to be included on some of these visits.

We took whole age groups (always at least one hundred children) on day-long Geography field trips to the Cotswolds, the Grand Union Canal and to the source of the River Thames.

Films were made at the School, both by our own Cine Club and by television companies using children as extras. There were fêtes on the fields to raise money for a good cause and there was Red Nose Day, which is part of Comic Relief, a national charity which raises funds for children. This national event occurred every few years throughout the country. Proceeds went to children's charities. We all wore red noses and dressed in theme outfits. The Chaplain looked more like a spider than a person. There was a sponsored spelling contest. I well remember a relay in which I was forced to take part - all of us had surnames starting with Mac. Our team was fancied, at least until the leg I had to run, which put an end to our winning chances. It was a day of great fun.

I was surprised when I first arrived to find the staff organised the children's travel at the start and end of term, accompanying children to and from the School. There were trips to Heathrow where check-in staff, seeing a particular child, would exclaim, "Oh no, not him again". This meant a free day for staff in London, finishing by returning on the School train. Once the point (switches) froze leading to a four hour trip which normally takes one. There was a late night trip to the railway station at the end of term. Each trunk, with its own specially-coloured label had to be checked. Not only checked, but its correct position on the various platforms checked, so trunks for Portsmouth wouldn't end up at Plymouth. I asked one boy, used to a long trip by aeroplane, why he always chose the centre seat in the long middle row. He replied "I get the liqueurs from the trolleys on both aisles". Away from our supervision, I hope good sense prevailed on the part of the aeroplane staff.

Later, when I had been at the School for over fifteen years, I intervened on a matter which affected the whole country and was never associated with the Dragon School. I took exception to advertisements for headmasters to I.A.P.S. prep schools. Most stated that the applicants must be graduates of United Kingdom universities. I couldn't really see why Monash or McGill degrees were inferior to St Andrews or Durham.

I wrote to the I.A.P.S (Incorporated Association of Preparatory Schools) Secretary and he raised the matter at the IAPS Council. They agreed with me. The requirement was stopped and schools were informed. Mind you, it was still necessary to look at each advertisement as some schools tried to ignore the Council's decision. I brought each to the attention of the Secretary and in the time the requirement was dropped. I felt that it was very important that these Headmasterships should be open to qualified and talented applicants from anywhere.

Staff sabbaticals too were an excellent idea. Once a year, starting in the 1970s and continuing during the 1980s, a member of staff would apply for a term "off" on full pay. Obviously we all wanted to take advantage of the opportunities offered for travel, for a special project, or to "recharge batteries". I travelled to Hawaii, and on to Australia, for my first visit. I was grateful for this opportunity.

The Headmasters, both Joc and Inky, realised just how important play was for the staff. In a residential school with many duties, it is easy to get into a rut. Then there will be sessions with colleagues complaining about the children and the Headmaster. Morale deteriorates. The staff retreat behind a wall of petty restrictions inflicted particularly on the children. All this can be very bad news.

Both Headmasters had an open door policy. It was possible for staff to visit them after hours, to meet socially, and often swap stories and talk of interests not connected with what one was doing. Many ideas came from this which could develop into something worthwhile down the line. Our special interests were encouraged. This might mean we wanted to be away occasionally during days of term time. Cover could be arranged.

Out of this we developed a Common Room where all adults working at the School could meet in the evening. We had our own committee to run it. Groups went off to play Skittles, to sporting matches as spectators, and to the theatre. The staff played cricket against other schools or clubs. Soccer and hockey teams took a similar interest. Some staff were very gifted athletically and were given permission to compete for their clubs and even in two cases for their country.

We gave lectures about our travels or special interests to the School. All this rubbed off on the children and enriched the atmosphere in the School.

24. School Fête. Will the slinky make it to the hole at the bottom? 1960s

25. Comic relief and Red Nose Day, 1992

26. Registering teddies for the Teddy Bear Show at the Dragon School, early 1990s

27. The Balloon Debate, Scots, 1992

CHAPTER 11

Australia

Early in the 1990s, I decided to try to teach for a year in Australia. The only way to do this was to try to arrange an exchange. Many Australians write to schools in England with the same intentions. From our files of such letters, I organised to go to Scots School in Albury.

This large town is twinned with the slightly smaller town of Wodonga on the south side of the Murray River. Together they are refereed to as Albury/Wodonga, with a combined population of more than seventy thousand. To the south of the Murray River is the State of Victoria, and to the north, the State of New South Wales. The Hume Highway connecting Melbourne with Sydney passes through the town and right beside the School.

To the south are some hills, where fruit trees grow around Beechworth, and on to the Ovens Valley. The Rutherglen Wineries and the wheat fields along the Murray River are to the west, and to the north, one is quickly in the outback with cattle and sheep. To the east, close to town is the Hume Dam and Lake. This water is gradually let out from the Dam for irrigation farther downstream. Further east and slightly south is the Kiewa River Valley leading to the Victorian Alps, home to the ski resorts of Falls Creek and Mount Hotham.

Albury is a long way from the New South Wales State capital of Sydney, so it is an administrative centre and home to a campus of Charles Sturt University.

Over many years, I had made a number of Australian friends. Taking full advantage of this, I arrived a week early in Melbourne to get acclimatised. Greg and Caroline met me when the train reached Albury. The took me to their home on Tribune Street, only one block from the School. It was August, mid-winter, with daffodils out in their garden.

After a two day introduction to Albury, they left for Oxford with their two children, Jeannie and Budi. The children fitted in very well at the Dragon School. As Greg came to grips with my teaching, Caroline, a computer expert, found work near Oxford for the year. We had done the exchange this way to fit in with the English school year which would be best for Jeannie and Budi.

The Scots School was formed in the early 1970s as a joining together of Albury Grammar (a boys' school founded in 1869) with Woodstock Presbyterian Girls' School, founded in 1894. The Scots School (motto "Fide Et Litteris" meaning " Faith and Learning") is not affiliated with any other Scots or Scotch schools or colleges, of which there are several in Australia. It is a Uniting Church school with a chaplain, and chapel built into the substantial school hall.

The School year runs from the end of January to mid-December, in four terms of nine and a half weeks each, with two week breaks three times a year. It is divided into primary (two hundred students) and secondary (five hundred students). Both are on the same site, but are separated by a large oval (playing field). The School is completely co-educational, and it is possible to attend it for thirteen years, as some have. The secondary school has boarders (160) and the division from primary to secondary comes at the end of year six when the children are twelve years old. I was assigned to the last year of primary, which included year one to six and a pre-primary year.

After two days in class with Greg, he left for England and I was on my own. Most of the classes in the primary are thirty or a bit under, but in year six there is a considerable intake of children from local State schools. There were forty five children in year six, but they were divided into two or three classes so the largest class I had was twenty five. They are streamed for Mathematics and Language. The curriculum is, not surprisingly, very different from what I had taught in England.

I had a very difficult time and without the sympathetic help of Meg, the teacher in charge of year six, John, the Headmaster, and one's colleagues, it might have ended in disaster.

Apart from the obvious cultural differences, the children were more than half way through the School year. They were used to Greg and his relaxed regime and I wasn't him. I wasn't familiar with Australian Geography and History and I had to try to cope with Craft and Cooking.

Often during my career, I solicited the help of parents, and soon a number came forward with the expertise and know-how for the Craft and Cooking. We made scones which were rock hard after cooking. The Home Economics room was well-equipped with six bays, each of which could accommodate four children. To keep order was a continuing struggle. One boy attempted to use an egg beater to rearrange a girl's hair, but only once! Our efforts to make good Australian pavlova were more successful.

My classroom, built in what had once been a factory warehouse, was large and well-supplied. The children from sub-primary to year two were in a purpose-built building which included a well-equipped library. Shortly after I arrived an adventure playground opened, which I enjoyed when I was on duty.

Colour and enthusiasm were everywhere. All children were divided into one of four houses for sport and some activities. Of the four "houses", three were named after tributaries of the Murray River: Mitta (blue), Kiewa (yellow) and Ovens (red). Snowy (green) was made famous by Banjo Patterson's poem *"The Man from Snowy River"*. I took soccer, T-ball, roller skating, athletics and supervised "Minkie" hockey and basketball, and for six months helped coach, organise and umpire an under-twelve cricket side called the City Colts.

Much less time was spent coaching and training at cricket, and more time playing, than in England. We played on Saturday mornings and were weaker than our opponents. Some potentially very good players had commitments elsewhere. We played on some very poor surfaces but we all enjoyed ourselves. Once a bail disappeared not more than ten feet behind the wicket keeper as the ground was so soft and absorbed it like quicksand. I was umpiring and ruled the batsman not out, quite correctly it proved, as the fallen bail could not be produced.

School games took place only on Friday afternoons during the week. The most amusing afternoon I had was spent coaching high jump. This took place indoors due to wet weather. There were two gymnasiums, both thirty five metres long and twelve metres wide, and were created by converting a warehouse storage area. This was not ideal. The beams were wide, and once, while supervising basketball, the balls all lodged on a beam ten metres up and had to be retrieved with a very long pole. And the roof leaked! I had been told that the girls should start the high jump at ninety centimetres.

On the run up, in bare feet, they slipped due to the wet floor. We dried it off with towels. We went down to eighty centimetres as no one had succeeded. At that point, loud music came through the thin wall of the gym next door, music for skipping practice. A hail storm opened up clattering onto the tin roof. The light switches were far away down a corridor and the lights took a long time to show anything. We went down to seventy centimetres. Some girls cleared this height to loud cheers, despite the noise, poor light, and wet floor. Any girl surviving this ordeal is on course for the 2004 Olympics!

We had a rotating timetable. Monday's lesson one week became Tuesday's the next and so on. In the primary all our lessons followed this pattern. This took some getting used to, but in the end I liked it. I taught Mathematics to the better half of the class and English to the second group. John, the Headmaster, took a remedial group "below" this second group.

Mathematics was supposed to happen four times per week and to last for fifty minutes per session. They had a workbook and an additional book for problems. I quickly discovered that they were poor at setting out their work and therefore were not in a position to do much useful working out. I changed the style of teaching immediately, and tackled the subject matter on a topic by topic basis. Homework was something that they were not used to doing. In the first week I gave a modest homework assignment to my Mathematics class and only two did anything. I did increase this total to half, but it was hard work. One father wrote to complain that homework interfered with his daughter's baby sitting duties.

Oral work in English was another challenge. I tried to act out a poem, *"The Highwayman"* by Alfred Noyes, with some success. We had a good balloon debate near the end of the School year. They were quite good at spelling, grammar and writing and could be outstanding at project work. I will have more to say about this later.

John, the Headmaster, supervised the children in a national competition called the "Tournament of the Minds". They practiced after school for six weeks and we went to Melbourne for the competition. No adult help could be offered to the problem. This was to write a play cast in a mythical Eastern European country where the Queen and her courtiers try to get the serfs to propel some food over the walls of the castle, which is under siege. As the food comprised six raw eggs in a container of nominal size, and had to reach two metres off the ground before landing on the hard ground of the castle courtyard, there were problems. A play had to be written, costumes had to be made, and above all the six eggs had to arrive unbroken. Eager inspectors examined the eggs for cracks and checked that they had not been hard boiled. As well as this, each team had to answer verbally a question which they had not been given in advance. For example, what would the world be like if there was no night? Apart from the lack of night clubs there was apparently little to say. Our team did not advance to the next round. The competition did encourage a spirit of enthusiasm among those who took part which was a good thing.

Lessons were all difficult. As there were no bells or signals to start and finish lessons, the times were very variable. As well as getting up and wandering around, the children threw paper, pencils and almost anything at each other; and even at the teacher. The best way to deal with this was to read aloud from the back of the classroom while children filled out blanks of a comprehension based on the reading. I hoped that they would tire of this and want to do something more productive. It was a true "blackboard jungle" and they clearly felt I wasn't delivering the goods. I tried everything. Sometimes it was a little better, sometimes not. I was nearly sixty and I realised that the youth and energy I had thirty years earlier was what was really needed.

There were "moments". We had an assembly once per cycle and we observed United Nations Day. I had a medal, a copy of which had been presented by the Secretary General of the United Nations to my cousin Ribby on his retirement from forty years as a press correspondent covering the United Nations. I explained its significance. Twenty four children dressed in national dress as many had family and ancestors who had come to Albury from outside Australia. Suzie was an American cow girl, Sarah, half-Indian, came in a sari, and Hannes who is Austrian, came in Liederhosen and one of those Tyrolian hats with a brush on the side.

At the end of one assembly a boy, Ian, asked me for my first impressions. I said that it was colourful, enthusiastic and the "soul" of the School was in good hands. A few days later I was visited after school by the Priest from St Patrick's Cathedral.

"What was all this about soul?" he asked. He said he had been bombarded by questions from young parishioners.

"Teach us about soul, Father", they said.

It made me think. I didn't want to be evasive but I had to admit I hadn't put much thought into the remark. Clearly I had started a number of children thinking. The Priest was very helpful when I explained what I had been doing and my problems. I have since been convinced that I was right and every school does have a soul. Since then, I have preached in Chapel using this as a theme. Schools have different versions of these - the practices, ethos and what each school stands for, what the School means to the children, teachers and those who know it. I have always been grateful ever since to the Priest from St. Patrick's and his young parishioners.

Exams came, were marked and reports written on individual slips. The dinner at the end of the year for the children graduating from year six had to be organised by the teachers. I wondered what we had to do. Yes, we were expected to raise all the money and to cook the meal. The children had a disco, a cake sale and a raffle. A committee of parents organised much of the cooking. The dinner, which included drinks before dinner and some funny presentations after, was a great success. The secondary school lent us their dining hall and all the crockery as well as the washing machine. I think that the children appreciated their graduation party more for having to work for it, rather than having it laid on for them. The boys were in tuxedos and the girls dressed formally which gave a certain atmosphere to the evening. The School year ends with a Christmas carol service held on a very hot evening and several levels of prize givings.

After the summer break, school resumed in early February. Little did I realise that now I would be regarded by the children and teachers as part of the establishment. Meg went off to teach Year One, as their regular teacher was having a baby. I was joined by Rosemary. She was under twenty five and recently married to a senior school teacher. She had taught before and had looked on at the primary school with some misgivings. She had a wonderful instinct and she was to prove one of my most valuable colleagues ever. We were a team and we "hit the ground running".

My lovely large sunny classroom had two doors and was used by many as a thoroughfare even during lessons. Children had been used to getting up and walking out at any time. Members of staff and parents would enter without asking or knocking, and if my back was to the door I wouldn't notice until they were in the middle of the room. Notices were read aloud, messages and gear delivered by parents, and even one child's pencil case gone through during my lesson by a teacher. Our letter to parents and another to all staff including secondary school teachers, put an end to all that. From February onward, I only remember one parent "trying it on" once and she was directed by me to the office by going outside and then to the front entrance.

Included also in our memos were guidelines for the staff regarding what was expected of the children in the way of behaviour, punctuality and homework. It worked. To parents, we told them to check that homework was done and to sign the diaries we had sent home each evening. They had very definite guidelines regarding what clothes, equipment and writing equipment was needed. Also we asked them to come to see us if they felt that there were any problems or misunderstandings.

Rosemary and I started the year with fifty children in year six which we divided into two classes of twenty five. I took all for Social Studies (History and Geography) and she took care of the Craft (cooking was replaced by "extra" craft at which she was very good).

The temperature as we unpacked books, put labels on everything, and received the children, was over 40°C. Male staff had to wear a tie at all times, but when the temperature reached 40°C we could take our ties off, this was a great relief. Gradually during the term the temperature dropped. I used to go for an evening dip in the Murray River (at 20°C) in order to sleep as I didn't have any air conditioning. There is a place along the River where a tree marks the spot where Hamilton Hume met William Hovell, an important meeting in Australian history, and it was there that I went for my evening swim. The children coped very well. It helped that the School swimming pool was just outside my classroom.

One of the first problems was some of the new intake. Fifteen boys and girls were new to the School. Their primary school advised their parents to send them to Scots for a year to get them used to the School and make their entry to the senior school easier. I suspected in some cases that they (the primary schools) were getting rid of some disruptive pupils. If they thought they were coming to us for extra discipline and toughening, then they were bound to be a problem. We were very firm regarding what was expected and had few problems. We were also very welcoming and took a great deal of trouble explaining how everything worked. This reduced uncertainty and I am sure helped.

Rosemary and I were very tough regarding homework. Any students who did not complete their homework assignments stayed after school the next day. We worked out a timetable for homework so it was spread evenly over the week. There was a further sanction known as "a Saturday morning". We informed the parents that their child would be required to attend school, in school uniform, for three hours from 9.00am. The key to this was that the giver of the sanction had to be at school to supervise it and to organise the work to be done. Four or five children came in the first term and one the second. The message was understood!

A Federal election took place during the first term to the Parliament in Canberra. We held a mock election with year six children representing the various political parties. At an election rally for all those in year three to six, the candidates pleaded for support. We then voted according to the Australian electoral rules, with single transferable votes. The children certainly had a lesson in civics learning how to rate the candidates in order on their ballot papers. Joshua, the Liberal candidate, was duly elected, but not without a fight. This sparked an interest in debating. Later in the year, we debated the following topics: *"What we learn at school is a waste of time"* (carried). *"Australia should become a republic by 2001"* (defeated) and that *"School days are the happiest days of our lives"* (defeated). We also entered a public speaking contest about how we are ruining our environment.

With four terms to the year, "events" could be more evenly spread, and did not pile up at Christmas and in June and July as in the northern hemisphere. Marks Twain's classic *"Tom Sawyer"* was being put to music by Lynn, the immensely talented Music teacher, with words by John, the Headmaster. This would be performed at the end of term two at the end of June, so casting took place at the end of term one. The terms of nine weeks were long enough. We all needed a break!

Our "camps week" came at the end of term one. Australian children go off to overnight camp at least once during the School year. Many schools maintain their own camps. We didn't, so we went to a camp called Borambola near Wagga Wagga about two hundres kilometres from the School. The camp is staffed and run by the Government of New South Wales. We signed up for a program of events and our fifty children shared the facilities with another school, staying in dormitories for two nights. and under canvas for another. We participated in organised activities in the evenings and did riding, grass skiing, archery, orienteering, fencing and nature study. It was wonderful for me to be back on horseback and to ride down to the Murrumbidgee River. We had to supervise the children at meals, laying up, serving, and all the cleaning up and stacking of dishes in the dishwashers. Our performance was inspected and commended on.

One side of this I simply hadn't realised. A parent who was a registered nurse accompanied us in her own car. She had pills, inhalers and many other necessary medical supplies. Living in a very dry climate with the air full of dust and pollen brings with it serious medical problems such as asthma. Only when we were all away overnight together was I aware of the extent of it all.

The group of children taken overall were much more interested and intelligent than those a year earlier. I had the better group for Mathematics and we were more or less finished the curriculum for the year during the second term. The written work was very good. To keep up interest we did some outdoor work - surveying and mapping - and some project work. As always Helen in the library was very helpful. The State Education Department provide a series of State and National competitions. The Mathematics Olympiad is run on a State-wide basis six times a year. The children tackle five problems in half an hour each time. It is a popular quiz with multiple choice questions based on no particular syllabus, and our children scored very well.

Wednesday was a day not included in the teaching cycle. I was able to get the use of the senior school laboratories for two forty minute periods. We were able to introduce the children to laboratory Science and they performed a number of simple chemistry and electricity experiments. They had to write about what they did with diagrams and illustrations for homework. There was also a State Science Quiz every month to stimulate interest.

I learned Australian History very fast. With the help of Helen in the Library, the children did some excellent project work. We also entered the State "Trivia Quiz" competition. Teams of four worked on a monthly quiz which was partly current affairs and partly general knowledge.

The English wasn't so easy. I had the less talented group and their spelling and grammar were weak. They wrote quite well, even if it wasn't technically correct. Some of the work was organised around a theme book (I used Colin Thiele's excellent children's books, *"Shatterbelt"* and *"Jodie's Journey"*) with comprehension, story writing and activities centred on these books.

Tom Sawyer rehearsals increasingly took time from lessons. I became involved as assistant artistic director. John, the Headmaster, increasingly went off to become stage manager. The play was well cast, the music and singing excellent, and it was all carried off with great enthusiasm. There were inevitably amusing incidents. One group of actors had to make a stage entry through a side door which was left unlocked. Someone had put a chair in the way so they couldn't get in. The play nearly ground to a halt as the stage manager ran through the audience to remove the chair and only in the nick of time.

Athletics and the cross country were very colourful with all the children in their house colours. Even the sub primary ran a couple of hundred metres across a field to show that they could take part. The parents all brought a picnic so we had a good time afterwards.

There were charity events too. We would sometimes have a "Sausage Sizzle" at lunch, with a gold coin ($1 and $2 coins) contribution to charity, and we collected far more than it cost to put on the event. We put on a Teddy Bear show on one occasion. Everyone in the School brought in their "Teds". These were divided into various categories, and after each was registered and an entry fee was paid, judging took place. There were prizes (horse racing-style numbered rosettes) for the most unusual, best dressed and most lovable Teds. Quite a good sum (over $200) was raised for charity.

Once a year, in March, the parents run a Summer Fair. There was a wide range of stalls and activities and they raised much needed funds for facilities in the School. I helped with the back up for a boy auctioneer who got rid of job lots of white elephant items (junk!) for a few dollars each.

There were many others events I was involved in and profited from. We toured a couple of Rutherglen wineries (with tasting!) and the forests (Monterey Pine imported from California grows fast here) and pulp mills for papermaking.

Discipline, performance and achievement held up very well. During my final weeks, events came on ever more rapidly until one day it was time to say good bye. Greg, Caroline, Jeannie and Budi returned and a friend from Melbourne came and took me away.

Probably the event which meant the most to me, was an expedition at the start of my final week. For several years there had been a Year Six day skiing expedition to Mount Hotham. We had heard that in recent years this had not gone well and had to be discontinued. Lack of control on the bus meant that some children had to receive medical treatment on arrival. As both Rosemary and I were keen on skiing and we felt that there would not be a discipline problem, we got permission from the Headmaster, to go. We sold the idea to the children who had to each raise $50 to come. I went to Mount Hotham during the previous school break to set everything up. It wasn't my first visit to this unusual resort. The "Town" is at the top of the mountain and skiers start by skiing down to the bottom to lifts which are in the valley below. The parents of Hannes (a boy in year six) built and owned "Zirkys", a combination ski shop and restaurant. They were to feed us and provide skis. The ski school were eager to help. One of our girls, Suzy, was not able to take part in most games as she was disabled. The head ski instructor had just been on a course to learn to teach skiers with disabilities and he couldn't wait to teach her.

Rosemary arrived with the bus. I was waiting with a stretcher to take away those injured during the journey. This brought a huge cheer. The children filed off to a snack, and to fit the skis, boots and sticks and all were off by mid-morning for a full day's skiing under instruction. We had some children who were so good they trained (not on this day) with the national team. Others were beginners who had never seen snow or skis before. It was a beautiful day and there was just enough snow.

Suzy had a great day. She held onto two ten foot poles and was slowly learning to walk on skis along the flat, with her chief instructor pulling the poles tucked under his arms. We had a large meal with the Zirknitzers after returning our skis and left, arriving two hours later back at school without a hint of any incident.

The trivia quiz contests continued after I left. One of our twelve teams of four, carefully balanced in ability and with two boys and two girls, attended the finals in Sydney in October. They didn't win but did reach the semifinals. This event (the overall competition) was sponsored and as a class (year six) we raised over $1000 for the Epilepsy Foundation.

I look back now on this period with great affection. Certainly the children had been great companions during my final six months. Many of the children had enjoyed and appreciated the events out of the classroom and I hope many of these lessons within as well. If one has taught at a school for a very long time, as I have, this sort of experience does bring home just how much exchange teachers owe to all those who make exchanges like mine possible. Memories are important but I gained a great deal in confidence and I felt that I was better prepared to meet whatever challenges I must face in coming years.

There are clear comparisons with my school in England. The curriculum at this level was quite flexible. The children and teachers did not have to face relentless content-based examinations. Exam results and league tables were not the goal of education. With an interested and talented group of children, it was possible to do so much more work which was interesting and ultimately valuable. The trouble can come, as I discovered when I first arrived, if there aren't guidelines and not enough is created to make the Schooling interesting, then it can all go so very soggy and wrong. Looking back now from retirement, I would have preferred to have worked under a system as the one I experienced in Albury, but I would have always been very dependant on the active participation of colleagues. Teaching in a tight little box just wouldn't have worked. It takes a special sort of Headmaster. John was such a man. Unfortunately he had so many interests that he was spread too thin. I admired him for what he did accomplish. Being out and about all the time doing things with the children was so very important. There wasn't a child whom he didn't know, and they knew him. He always said he was miscast. He is a practising Uniting Church Minister and he had been asked by the Church to run the primary school. Shortly after I left, he became the School Chaplain, more his vocation but I gather he is still often seen with a hammer and nails in one hand and a piece of play scenery in the other.

28.   Joshua gives a lecture, 1993

29.   United Nations Day, 1992

30. Year 3 reads to Year 6, 1993

31. Mt Hotham, 1993

32. Suzy and her own chief instructor, 1993

33. Caroline, Head Girl, Scots Primary School
Swimming pool, 1992

CHAPTER 12

Expeditions Overseas

I was fortunate to be part of nearly fifty expeditions in my time. Inky once said to Guv and me that no prizes could be given at school for any exploits on any overseas trips as some children were always excluded. Their parents could not afford the cost. To pay the fees was all that they could manage. He was absolutely right to say this.

The Paris trip was low cost. We took a party of no more than twenty five boys, girls, matrons, staff and a few parents. The purpose was to have a French experience with a very good and worthwhile time in the capital. Even in the 1980s we kept the cost below £250 (total). The group travelled out on a Monday and came back on a Friday, giving us four nights in Paris.

Perhaps strangely the most difficult part of this trip was the evening meal and the accommodation. The French consider that foreign groups should stay in a hostel or students' hotel and eat evening meals in an assembly line cafeteria. One year we had to do things this way and it wasn't pleasant. In student accommodation, one has no control over other groups or their leaders. Part of the experience should be staying in a French hotel and enjoying the amenities including a "Petit Dejeuner". Very good inexpensive hotels do exist - the problem is to find them. Insisting on one person in each bed can be a problem - they have ideas about stacking bodies side by side in a wide bed like bottles in a wine rack!

Restaurants have a certain special atmosphere - white table cloths covered with clear plastic - their own special lighting and sometimes music. One of us usually travelled out a few months ahead to agree on the timing, prices and set the menu. A soup or crudités, main course with chips, a salad and a dessert - preferably something typical like creme brulé plus lots of orange and coke to drink. The best arrangement we ever made was organised by a school governor when we were classified as a religious group: this meant we could eat at a nunnery! Here there was a vow of silence until a group of pilgrims came to eat. Then the nuns had a wonderful time with the children. They took them to the kitchen in the cellars and even let them ride the dumb waiter up to the dining area. French conversation flowed in all directions. The adults had a glass of wine the first night with the Mother Superior in her office.

We divided into smaller groups for sight seeing. Groups of ten travelling on a set route, using a "tariff reduit" according to the handwritten coupon, travelled at minimal cost on the Metro. We visited many of the well-known sites including Notre Dame, Sacre Coeur (at both we climbed onto the roof), the Eiffel Tower, the Invalides, the Louvre and many lesser-known museums, including the Cluny and Carnavalet. Near the Sacre Coeur in the Place de Terne, the children sat for artists who sketched portraits of them (we always agreed on a maximum price in advance). On the last morning we finished with the Science Museum, full of static electricity.

The Metro, as well as being our main mode of transport, was also where we made a unique visit. Not only did we see the control centre where on a huge wall one follows the progress of each train, but we also rode in a cab with the driver on a fast suburban R.E.R (Reseau Express Régional) train. I didn't like visiting the sewers (yes, there is a guided tour), or the catacombs (too many skulls and piles of bones).

The small local bakeries go underground. Once below (and very cramped for spectators), we shared in the baking of baguettes, preparation of croissants and even the difficult art of casting the chocolate, thin and uncracked, for the Easter bunnies.

The whole exercise of preparing the lunch had educational value. Two to four children, each with an adult, peeled off early from the morning visits and into a market. There they bought baguettes, paté, meats, cheese, butter, oranges, chocolate and soft drink as well as tomatoes, cucumbers and anything else which would add to our lunch. Then they set up camp in outdoor public gardens with a tap and benches, and laid out the lunch. There were strict rules about cleaning and washing one's hands and the food. No corkscrew was allowed and we bought cutting boards, sharp knives, some spoons and spreading knives with us from England. When the main part of the group arrived, the lunch was ready.

At Versailles, the Etoile du Sud restaurant had a back room (provided we ordered their drink) for groups with picnics. We were under cover, sometimes a necessity. After the lunch we toured the Palace, Grand Trianon, Petit Trianon and Marie Antoinette's Hameau (children's playground) before regrouping at the Etoile du Sud for some biscuits and drink and then the trip "home".

The trip had a sort of mystique. In the Musée Grevin (the wax museum and French equivalent of Madame Tussauds) was a hall of mirrors and conjurers show. That was in a way what the trip was all about, bizarre, fun, interesting, and cultural with much good exercise and eating.

There was usually something unexpected. Julia, a mother delivering her son Hugh to our hotel, having travelled from Luxembourg and not London, came across a situation. Several of our children were practising their skills as lift operators. Madame the Concierge was "white" with rage. Julia sorted out the children, freeing the lift for other guests. Madame assumed that Julia was a member of staff, obviously one with 'grip'. She could never understand where Julia had gone after this.

On another occasion, in a hotel which had known better times, Edward spotted that the intercom telephones could be programmed to ring all the other rooms. On the morning of 1 April he rang most other rooms early and told them to send one member to the kitchen where the petit dejeuner was being provided on a tray, as breakfast would have to be taken in the rooms, the lounges were unavailable. Soon a long line formed. The hotel was slow at picking up the significance of the date.

One year, Maxwell, a boy from our trip, returned the following week and showed his parents' business clients around Paris. They said it was a better and more interesting tour than anything they had had with a professional guide in other European cities!

Another low-cost trip was that to Brussels. This was more high-powered and intended to educate. The purpose was to visit the institutions of the Common Market; the Commission, Council and Parliament. We had briefings and sat in the Council Chamber as if we were heads of Government, and had Council proceedings explained to us. We had a session with one of the Commissioners, Sir Leon Brittain, and the chance to ask him questions. We stayed with friends, old boys of the School working in Brussels, and ate out near the Grand Palace. The visit included N.A.T.O Headquarters and an additional excursion to the site of the Battle of Waterloo.

There were trips I accompanied to France to the First World War battlefields. A group of teaching colleagues had a great interest in these terrible events. Edward, the leading expert, wrote two anthologies of poems, one for each World War. I well remember once during a reconnaisance when a small group of three colleagues decided one evening that there must have been a dressing station at a certain location. We set out early soon after dawn so as not to attract attention. On our hands and knees, we searched and dug down slightly using knives. Sure enough, buttons and other insignia emerged, left where uniforms had been torn and cut off so wounds could be quickly treated.

Several times in late August, we went to the Somme with children and their families. It was delightfully informal. We spent time in certain fields looking for shrapnel balls and we had "night" manoeuvres. At dusk we waited at a location which had been in "No Man's Land" at the time of the British attack in 1916. On one occasion I touched an electric cattle fence, gave a loud moan, and it was assumed that I had "bought it"!

When it was finally totally dark, some of us "defended" trenches. Pairs of children taking advantage of any dips in the landscape, grass and bushes slowly advanced. The object was to reach the trench unspotted. Plastic bags were tied to bushes behind the trench. Once I was completely fooled. One member of the advancing pair leapt up in the air shouting, "I surrender". I was distracted just long enough for his "mate" to get around me and to capture a plastic bag.

We visited locations where famous battles and incidents took place. At Vimy Ridge, using tunnels and "Blitzkrieg" tactics, the Canadians broke through the German lines. At the Newfoundland park some signals were misunderstood and the Newfoundland regiment advanced and were nearly all cut down.

We knew exactly where the Lancashire Regiment attacked across a field from a sunken road near Beaumont Hamel. Unfortunately the Hawthorn Crater on a ridge commanding the battlefield, and the result of many weeks of digging and mining, was blown ten minutes too soon. There is a cemetery to the Lancashires beautifully maintained by the Commonwealth War Graves Commission in the field where they advanced.

As well as much walking in what is now quite empty and beautiful rolling landscape, we learned a great deal.

For over forty years I was involved with the Dragon School's skiing expeditions to Davos in Switzerland. It all started as a group of about thirty five going to a small but sympathetic hotel. Herr Martin Lohner, a large gruff man with great charm and a terrible temper when he wanted to use it, made us very welcome. We continued to use his hotel, in later years run by his son Edouard (known as Herr Lotion), for thirty five years. The stories were legendary. For the first dozen years other skiers were there with us but there was surprisingly little friction.

Once a party of six Dutch ladies were horrified on arrival to find the hotel full of school children. They complained loudly, but with no result. It never paid to get excited with Herr Lohner about anything. Rather eccentrically, the ladies soon had their chess sets out for an evening session. Some of the boys took an interest and were soon advising the ladies on possible future moves. By the third night, the ladies waited in anticipation surrounded by mountains of the best Swiss chocolates. One lady confided to me that the standard of the boy's chess was better than the chess club at home. There were no further problems.

On another occasion, I was trapped in a corner of the sitting room by a furious Herr Lohner. The children had been snowballing the front of the hotel, a window had cracked and would cost an enormous sum to repair. I pointed out that Herr Lotion, his son, who was then the same age as our children, had been among the snowballers. "Is that so?" Resistance crumbled.

It wasn't all as easy at that. Once at the Olympic-sized municipal swimming pool across the road from the hotel, one of our children was assaulted by an attendant. He was no doubt provoked, as instructions in the pool had not been followed. We always had an adult with our children, but he was by the pool and the trouble developed elsewhere near the changing area. Alas the police had to become involved. The case came to court but was dismissed because there were no witnesses. The next year, I asked the tourist director, who had been very helpful to us throughout, what had happened to the attendant. I was told he was on permanent garbage collection so no more harm could be done. Justice had been served after all.

We did actually do some skiing, in fact a very great deal! No matter how heavy the duties of the organisers, we always skied all day until 4.00pm when January darkness descended. The resort was ideally situated to appeal to every level of skill and interest. The children were all in ski classes to suit their experience and ability. Lessons were given to the beginners, with combinations of piste and off-piste skiing with a bit of instruction and jumping for the more advanced. Parents sometimes joined the lessons and there were days when they took their children skiing en famille.

Gradually the numbers coming each year increased: in time we numbered a hundred. We still had many unaccompanied children. The parents were a great asset and entered willingly into the spirit of the trip. This was to ski as much and in as great a variety of ski areas as possible. More and more the parents took on duties. Some would go as "Tail End Charlies" with the fast ski classes, to help the Swiss ski school instructors. Others offered and helped with after dinner games and activities. This included tobogganing and ice skating.

To organise each day was a massive task. No groups were ever the same from day to day. New technology in drawing up lists - the portable laptop - came into use. We did have accidents with bone breaks, sprains, bruises and torn ligaments. We did our best to avoid these and as equipment improved, with better safety bindings, there were fewer accidents. The ski shop was excellent and did everything it could to help. In time a mountain pass was issued for one price covering all lifts and trains.

I well remember one year when a train containing eighty Dragons arrived at Davos Dorf station. In five minutes all children and adults had their ski identity pass, instructions on where to go to the ski shop, had put their luggage on a waiting truck and were off to the hotel. Everyone knew their hotel room number and had a bus pass and map of Davos. All this was made possible because a small advance party which had been at the hotel for several days, skied down the longest continuous downhill run in the world (Davos to Kublis - thirteen kilometres in length) to meet the mountain train one hour before its arrival in Davos Dorf.

Parents were fascinated with all aspects of the ski trip and we attracted talented and willing allies from among them to help in many ways. They helped us to form the Dragon Ski Club, independent of the School with its own constitution and directors. This made the running of this trip by the School organisers much easier.

A group of staff and parents formed the Black Truffle Ski Club. The Black Truffle had won his name because he had a black ski suit, gloves and hood. He often fell in deep snow and had to be dug out by the rest of us as pigs smell out truffles in France. Other "officers" included the Keeper of the Torch, the Bearer of the Rope, the Keeper of Sanity, the Pink Tulip and the Blue Onion. This group of wizards surely would have attracted interest from Harry Potter. The Club met at a headquarters. This was a small and remote mountain restaurant served by a vivacious Yugoslav waitress called Dragitza. There were many obscure Club rules which I couldn't understand, but they did organise a superb annual treasure hunt.

In the treasure hunt, we were divided by age and years of experience at skiing so we were all in teams of equal ability. Bonus points were awarded for colourful outfits and names were given such as the *Accidents, Family Rows, Tangerines* and *Bombers*. We were given sheets of clues as we set out in the morning. We had about five hours to scour mountain huts, advertising signs, ski lifts and ski runs for answers. There were ski runs we had to complete to be able to answer most of the questions. On the course at some stage we had to call in at headquarters to obtain Dragitza's signature. The children all took part and had a wonderful time.

Progress was quite slow a the team had to be together at all times and some skiers were little better than beginners. The members of the Committee skied as "Marshals" to make sure we were always obeying Club rules. We finished at the Strela Alp Mountain restaurant, where teams reported to the Committee, had our Alpen coffees, soft drinks and apple strudel. Later in the evening prizes were awarded in the hotel.

The motto of the Dragon Ski Club is "Ab Schwendi Ad Schwendi" which means from hut to hut. The mountain huts were at various levels and could be reached by mountain transport as well as by ski. The ski classes, for all children, were with a ski school guide and with one of our adults as the "Tail End Charlie", stopped for lunch at a schwendi (hut). Ten francs didn't go far so one year we asked for a plate of spaghetti, chips and a drink to be available for less. This was advertised as a "Dragon Special" and attracted interest from other skiers as well.

We took part in local events. We belonged as a club to the Ski Club of Great Britain (S.C.G.B.). More experienced children entered the Marden Club Races and we tried out the S.C.G.B. bronze and silver tests with much success.

Most years we were able to enter teams into the Beat Fopp Cowbell Marathon Derby. Mr. Fopp was a local businessman. As a boy he had belonged to the S.C.G.B and won many of their races. When he was older, he decided to sponsor a new kind of contest under the S.C.G.B umbrella. This competition was for skiers with some experience. Many teams of two from our ski club entered hoping to win in one of the catagories: best time, under twenty eight combined ages, or over one hundred combined ages. We started at a mountain restaurant and had to ski as many different runs as possible in six hours, finishing in Wolfgang in a hotel in the valley. A knowledge of probable lift delays, queues and railway and bus timetables was as important as an ability to ski. Runs repeated were not counted and the use of taxis or cars not included on our mountain pass was not allowed. In some years, Prince Charles competed so giving the event a sort of Royal Stamp of approval.

I remember arriving at Klosters Station with Adam, a good skier, but slow to move otherwise. The train was leaving so a couple of us lifted him onto the train with his skis still attached to the disapproving stare of the conductor who thought we were quite mad. Mr. Fopp was most generous with the prizes and almost everyone came away with something.

Alas Michael C., one of our staff members, died between ski seasons. In his memory we awarded each year the Moo Cow (Michael's nickname) Bell. This went to someone who made a unique contribution. Michael liked the unusual, the bizarre and above all those with a sense of humour.

Nicholas came into lunch one day at the beginners slope restaurant in tears. I asked him what had happened. He said his skies had come off. There was nothing unusual about that. They had slid downhill. I asked him if he had gone down after them. He replied that they weren't there.

"Where have they gone", I asked

"Into the river and they floated away", he said.

One must be prepared to believe almost anything! In fact he was "spot on". We went immediately along the trail by the river and found the skies on a small rapid, half a mile down stream. (Nicholas, whose exploits came many years before the Moo Cow

Bell, would have been a worthy winner.)

Andrew was a worthy winner. He is a financial expert and was skiing with his daughter Henrietta and his son Hugo. On arrival we gave everyone dyno labels to stick on skis, boots and sticks. Andrew neglected to put his name on the boots. At the mountain top, they wouldn't fit his skis. Fortunately Hugo was not far away so they swapped the same size boots and all was well. Andrew then fell off the T-bar lift. This is not unusual as they can be most challenging. He stood up, and spotted another skier with a free T-bar slot beside him. He lunged for this, broke off the T-bar and again, with the unsuspecting brief partner, plunged into deep snow. Later that morning, when we arrived at a schwendi, Andrew misjudged the approach and went crashing into the hut with skis on, and all just as someone opened the door. We picked him up, shook the snow off, got him a hot drink and set off again. Alas Andrew hadn't put his name on his skis either so he had to try on fifty pairs of skis, all of which he said resembled his own. Finally we were off. At the bottom we took the cable car. Just as we were about to get on, Andrew remembered he had left his gloves on a ledge at the far end of the waiting room. The silent glass panel of the cable car slid shut, condemning Andrew to wait for the next car. He was a worthy winner, but alas he had to return to his financial affairs in London before the presentations. His son, Hugo, was understandably reluctant to come up to receive the prize.

We certainly had our fun. Many adults and children developed a life-long love of skiing. There were some prizes for down downhill and slalom races reorganised, or were part of the SCGB silver and bronze tests. Inky was right to insist that if we gave prizes for these races, they had to be awarded in Davos, and not back at school as part of our main prize day.

The day of departure was always a dangerous time. All bills had to be paid, equipment returned and hopefully everyone could gather at the hotel at the appointed hour. We all skied on the last day as we left in the late afternoon. We had some breakages on the last day but somehow these could be patched up well enough so we could leave. Once, Parki, one of our regular adults, arranged to ski down literally right to the bus just as it was leaving. He had his own ski boots and sticks which fitted into a special case which a friend brought to the bus. The same friend put his bags on the bus for him. It made life much easier as an organiser to arrange to leave the next day. This was true except in one way. No matter how hard the adult volunteers tried, scouring every corner of every room, there was always lost property left behind, usually unmarked.

I finish this chapter with some suggestions on how to organise a successful trip overseas. We always tried to do most of the details ourselves as in that way we had more control over what happened. We did have a travel agent for air, train or coach journeys but we learned it was better to deal direct. In this way the price could not differ from what was agreed.

The most important lessons I learnt from these trips were to make sure that the trip had a purpose, was affordable, had a thorough reconnaisance in advance, had good accommodation and food, good staffing, clear guidance about cost, dates, items required and expected behaviour whilst on the trip, and that all travel and other details are carefully checked. Above all, a de-briefing after the trip should always be held to ensure that no mistakes are repeated.

34. Madurodam, Scheveningen, Holland, 1967

35. A Schwerdi visit

36. The Black Truffle Treasure Hunt in action

CHAPTER 13

Conclusion - The "Extra Ten Percent"

Now forty years on from my time at Bishops University with Dr. Jefferis (Jeff), working one morning a week at Fairview Heights Elementary School (part of the public school system in Halifax, Nova Scotia), I rack my mind for pointers which will help with Katie Lee's spelling. Make it interesting. Have a plan and routine but always something new each week. For Shea and his lack of ability at tables, form a table square, illustrate the beauty of numbers with primes and factors.

It is a new challenge. Fairview Heights is close to where those whose bodies were rescued from the sinking Titanic lie in peace. It is voluntary work in retirement. There are other deserving jobs I could do, but as I am a teacher it seems reasonable to want to do something where I am wanted and appreciated.

We tend to look back through our careers through rose-tinted glasses seeing only the great events. What is really important is the day to day struggle to put across the teaching. Be organised and do have, as Jeff insisted, a lesson plan. If it doesn't work then try something else. Some years and classes are more difficult than others. Work to what you are capable of and are happy with. This is why I now volunteer to do tutoring. There comes a point when one is just too old to face a full classroom day in, day out. I have described events and values as I saw them during my teaching career. The Dragon School was hard to leave. I went on two exchanges, one to New York City and the other to Australia. I taught at Sept Iles for two years and had one year each at Trinity College School and at Appleby College, both near Toronto. But I always returned to the Dragon. It had a compelling interest for me. As I became older I was in many ways more valuable to the School. I organised and ran activities and events, but at the same time I became less and less effective on the sports fields.

As the School was large as prep schools go, there was always something new to try. I don't suppose that my teaching ever stayed the same for two consecutive years. New activities came along and together with colleagues we tried to give them a chance. It was sometimes hard but necessary to give up important responsibilities such as running the Christmas Charity Sale, but for one's sanity, essential to do so!

Another vital feature was the support given to me (and others) by the School and Headmaster for new initiatives like orienteering and public speaking, once they had been thoroughly worked out and explained. All colleagues, be it in Music, Art, Carpentry, or Chess, had similar support. A sense of continuity was in existence. This meant that it was expected that new and exciting events and activities would occur and old ones not necessarily go on forever.

All this had an impact on the world outside. Everyone wanted "in"! Children couldn't wait until they were old enough to enter. In early September droves of children already at the School, on and off bicycles, followed us around the playground in anticipation of the start of the School year.

Until the early 1980s, we had never had young ladies as stooges. Elwyn was the older sister of a boy at the School. Inky thought "she" was a young man so took her on sight unseen. It is to the credit of both that this proved a great success. The ice was broken, and since then a long line of lady stooges has passed through the School. Inky had a great talent with women. They never felt threatened by him and he had such tact and charm that they always ended up doing what he wanted. The School was lucky to have had both Inky and Guv at this time. Guv too was very good with women in the same sort of way. Society was changing and women were becoming considered as equals and could do most of the jobs considered in an earlier era as being the exclusive preserve of men.

I also learned that it is up to the individual to become accepted. There were inevitably back in the 1960s comments about "colonials". I never took these seriously. One day towards the end of my first year, I was heard to say to Clarkie, "The goddam mail truck is late again." This caused a certain amount of mirth as the English call this sort of vehicle "the post van". This story helped to break the ice if there ever was any.

Many of us were deeply involved with classroom teaching. As we gained in experience, we became more aware of our inadequacies. We did our best to correct these, to improve our methods by attending outside courses, and by making sure that, at whatever level, the children understood.

It was said of Joc that he taught us that the children mattered most and I think that that was the main reason that they remained so loyal to the School. When they became adults it was this memory of themselves as children that really mattered. They were allowed and even encouraged to remain children until it was time to grow up.

Most were very sensitive about good behaviour. They had fun, did their own thing, but knew when not to interrupt or put on "airs". This could only come through respect.

Many of the children achieved a great deal in later life. I can't help but think that some of it came from their time at school. It was often those you didn't expect to achieve much. The point is that hopefully they were not "driven" to reach measurable goals all the time. One would hope that there was no great emphasis on winning teams and high academic grades. In fact, because they look back with affection, they were well on their way to achieving their own "ten percent". In life, that extra little bit matters. One advantage of a large school is that a wide range of interests are offered. Hopefully every child could find somewhere where each could excel. It was in many cases well away from the classroom.

Parents expected their children to pass their exams. During my time at the Dragon School these exams were largely, though not completely, content based. With motivated and determined children with good work habits, this went well, but too often exam requirements left little scope for stimulating and valuable learning which didn't need to be examined. This is why I said that I found my second stint in Australia so rewarding. Eventually exam results matter however. To raise standards just on the basis of results and league tables undermines confidence and can instill a loathing for a subject and the teacher. I used to get great credit for pushing some incompetent Mathematics students through the Common Entrance Exam. Looking back, I feel I must have put some off.

The Dragon School was to me a very great school. If one examined the administration and how it was run, one might conclude that it couldn't be managed and was out of control. The fact that it wasn't, and that it ran very well, and achieved so much, was a credit to the teachers and the School. The key was teachers who came and stayed a long time. They were committed. In no other school I came across were so many so committed. The children soon pick up if one is not giving one hundred and ten percent. Anyone who wants to become a teacher must remember this.

I am not a believer in "born" teachers. Too many of this kind are good politicians who know how to impress, obviously with possible advancement on the horizon. Good teachers are always learning and they must work closely with colleagues to be successful. You could fill a school with proven good teachers and not have a good school at all. This may sound ridiculous. I well remember a Headmaster who had two phone numbers, one through his secretary and the other direct to his desk. His secretary was fierce, rude and kept people away from her boss. To have the Head's direct number was a plus. The point is that all those behind the scenes who do all those vital secretarial and bursarial jobs are tremendously important and should be recognised for this. The Dragon School had a "works" outing for them to the Henley Regatta each year. The stooges and matrons were essential too. Without them, a boarding school like the Dragon School could not operate.

Three of the schools I taught in, Trinity, Appleby and the Buckley School in New York, I have left out. This is because I didn't make a notable contribution. This isn't to say that they were not good schools, they were. However I don't remember enough to make any contribution worthwhile. In teaching one can get enormous personal pleasure and self-esteem from helping and teaching others. This also gives a boost to the respect for those who are older in society. Unfortunately, in today's world, such people when they are retired are dismissed as irrelevant and useless. This, of course, is entirely wrong though I do admit that some of us can be pretty boring when we pontificate about the good old days!

To finish, just a short description of the Joint Education Trust (J.E.T.). After retiring, I spent five valuable years helping this important charity.

J.E.T. was started thirty years ago under the Chairmanship of Sir Douglas Bader to identify families where children were not reaching their full potential, whether because of problems at home or some sort of disability. Often the children were traumatised through no fault of their own and some were literally at risk. J.E.T. places these children in schools best able to provide the necessary security and educational facilities to meet their needs, and locates and arranges funding for these places.

I have visited over one hundred schools in the United Kingdom looking for sympathy and support. We are the only charity aimed at children seven to eleven years old. Also I have visited families whose children are seeking our support.

Always I first see the Head of the school. Confidentiality is a key element. Often only the Principal or Head knows the family situation and the fact that J.E.T supports a child is kept out of the public view. There may be financial problems. The families may have little money which is another reason that we are called in to support the child. For this very good reason I would not want to give any account of schools visited and what happened.

One vacation break I was returning from Norway with Splinter. We had a long and delayed trip across England to Oxford. It was dusk when we arrived. There was a light on in Inky's drawing room. We went over to see if he was there. Immediately we were made welcome and sandwiches and hot drinks appeared and the conversation flowed. It was all about good times during the break.

On many occasions I would return to Gunga Din where I was living before becoming Housemaster. Guv was in residence. His curries were legendary. There was always an extra plateful for me no matter what was the state of the evening. Again the conversation flowed. Sometime later the pavlova and cheese were produced.

During my years in Australia we were never too busy to mark an event at morning recess. During lunch break and just after school, there would be an anniversary, birthday or the Melbourne Cup to celebrate. Drinks, cheese, chicken bits and sandwiches as well as a cake. It was good to relax especially if we were in and out of the staff room on duty.

All these ingredients were a crucial part of that "extra ten percent". In an era where the job description is paramount, these extra ingredients were all welcome reminders of a more relaxed, caring and happier time. That is what it was like and possibly most of us were not aware of the little bit extra we all put in.

If there are any profits from the sale of this book I would like to make ongoing contributions to J.E.T. and to the Lynam Educational Trust. The Trust enables deserving children whose families can't afford today's school fees to attend the Dragon School.

CHAPTER 14

Epilogue

Readers will have immediately noticed that this book ends when Inky and Guv left, and a new Headmaster arrived, despite the fact that I continued on the staff for a few more years. This is not intended as any disrespect to the subsequent period, nor indeed its main characters. Instead, it is an acknowledgement that the retirement of those two remarkable men did bring the era about which I chose to write to an emphatic end. Indeed, the years which followed will be better understood if told by some future author in their proper context.

When I left the Dragon School in 1994, it was with a conscious decision to stay away for several years. The School had been such a central part of my life that I needed to find a new focus. However, that having been achieved, I now return to the School at the generous invitations of the current Headmaster and governors.

As I am always being asked what I think of the School now, I can happily report that it seems in excellent health and I thoroughly enjoy my visits. Yes, of course things change, but then they always need to do so. The social and educational environments in which schools exist constantly evolves and so they must too. The only issue is to best handle and manage such change - a subject that gives my profession endless hours of vigorous debate.

That said, I still maintain that the Dragon School is a special place and that some of the essential magic which we all felt persists to this day. A simple story can perhaps best testify to this.

Very early in this book, I told the story of my friend Alexis's first encounter with the Headmaster, Joc Lynam. He had been told to present himself at a certain part of the School first thing in the morning while I was teaching. A maintenance man was clearing out a room I had said was the Headmaster's study. When Alexis, a very young and junior master at a Canadian boarding school, asked where was the study, and where could the Headmaster be found, this man dressed in several sweaters containing many holes replied, "This is it and I am he".

This had started a long association with the School. Alexis for many years brought students to visit Oxford from his Canadian school, then introduced his wife and his own children. He was good at getting himself invited to the Headmasters Conference as the Canadian guest.

Many years later, now himself a distinguished retired Headmaster, Alexis returned to Oxford and again visited the School, though this time to borrow a desk for an apartment in which he was staying. At the School he was directed to the playground, where he saw a neatly turned-out man wearing a smart anorak, who was busy moving a couple of rubbish bins and picking up some pieces of stray paper. Assuming him to be one of the famous maintenance men, Alexis politely asked where he could find the person with the desks, and he was similarly courteously directed to the right office. Having found his contact and sorted out the desk, he was asked how he had found the right place. Alexis explained about the man picking up and moving the bins and rubbish and was asked if he had given a name.

Well, he was a very self-effacing man, Alexis replied, and I think he said his name was Roger. Roger was in fact the present Headmaster.

Nearly forty years separate those two events, but clearly the Dragon School continues to select headmasters who are perfectly happy to muck in when the occasion demands it, but can also manage and lead what I, and many others whose lives it has touched, consider to be a quite remarkable school.

The school motto is "Arduus Ad Solem" which means "Striving for the Sun". I now know what that means.